Alcyon Ferreira de Souza Junior

Cyber Security

Alcyon Ferreira de Souza Junior

Cyber Security

Brazilian politics and international experience

ScienciaScripts

Imprint
Any brand names and product names mentioned in this book are subject to trademark, brand or patent protection and are trademarks or registered trademarks of their respective holders. The use of brand names, product names, common names, trade names, product descriptions etc. even without a particular marking in this work is in no way to be construed to mean that such names may be regarded as unrestricted in respect of trademark and brand protection legislation and could thus be used by anyone.

Cover image: www.ingimage.com

This book is a translation from the original published under ISBN 978-620-2-19039-8.

Publisher:
Sciencia Scripts
is a trademark of
Dodo Books Indian Ocean Ltd. and OmniScriptum S.R.L publishing group

120 High Road, East Finchley, London, N2 9ED, United Kingdom
Str. Armeneasca 28/1, office 1, Chisinau MD-2012, Republic of Moldova, Europe
Printed at: see last page
ISBN: 978-620-7-30715-9

I dedicate this work to my family and fiancée, who are always by my side, and especially to God, who always guides my steps.

"Success is built at night! During the day you do what everyone else does." Roberto Shinyashiki

There has been an increase in cybercrime and a search for government or private company assets that have failed security and support critical infrastructure services. This paper addresses the issue of cyber security and its importance on the world stage. Cyberspace contains various information and critical infrastructure services that must be given special attention by the actors involved. In this context, cyber security policies are fundamental, as they establish the regulatory framework from which actions will be established and monitored, roles and responsibilities are defined. This study evaluates Brazil's Cyber Defence Policy (CDP) with the aim of contributing to the enrichment of discussions on this topic. To this end, the cyber security policies of other countries are analysed and their guidelines are compared with the PCD. The relevance of the results is checked with an expert in the field. The work also presents aspects of the UCP that deserve attention.

Keywords: Cyber Security Model. National defence strategy. Cyber Defence Policy.

SUMMARY

CHAPTER 1

INTRODUCTION

Irrefutably, companies are increasingly using the Internet to utilise and provide services and information to their customers and suppliers. In order to coordinate and integrate all internet service initiatives in the country, so as to promote technical quality, innovation and the dissemination of the services offered, the Brazilian Internet Steering Committee (CGI.br) was created by Presidential Decree[0] 4.829 of 3 September 2003. In terms of the proportion of companies using e-government services, the CGI.br (2012) survey shows that companies have used some e-government service. To show the study carried out, we have a graph available at CGI.br (2012, p. 219), with the proportion of companies that have used some e-government service. In the last 12 months, only one transaction is among the main forms of online interaction with the government: online payments of taxes and fees (63 per cent). The other alternatives are consultations or searches on websites. In addition, 27 per cent of the companies interviewed said they had not carried out any of the transactions covered by the question. As can be seen in Figure 1:

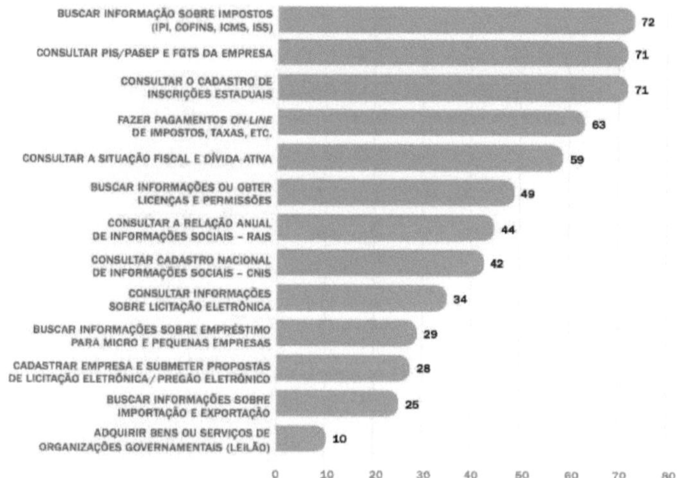

Figure 1 - Proportion of companies using e-government services in 2012

Source: CGI.br (2012)

Figure 1 shows the percentage of companies that carry out transactions with the government. It is possible to see the high proportion of companies that use Internet services in connection with their legal obligations. This use of government services on the Internet must, in turn, be accompanied by the maintenance of information security and confidentiality. The World Wide Web is also used by a number of national public bodies. This data also needs to be protected to ensure its confidentiality. Figure 2, drawn up by the Centre for the Study of Security Incident Response and Treatment in Brazil

(CERT.br), shows information on attacks, invasions, incident reports and information theft on the Internet, reported between January 2012 and December 2012. It can be seen that the denial of *service* attack, which aims to make several simultaneous connections in order to overload and temporarily remove the service provider from the network, has an almost negligible number of occurrences compared to other types of attack. On the other hand, the scanning of network assets and their services (*scan*), which tests the logical ports of remote servers, accounted for approximately fifty percent of the total attacks in the period analysed. Both attacks invalidate service providers by overloading them. Fraud is a type of incident that is an illicit or bad faith scheme created for personal gain using email and other means of digital communication. Web incidents are websites that contain fake content in order to pass themselves off as a real organisation's page, with this technique the perpetrator manages to steal information from the visitor. In an intrusion, the hacker accesses their target's system to view, copy or even delete their target's information.

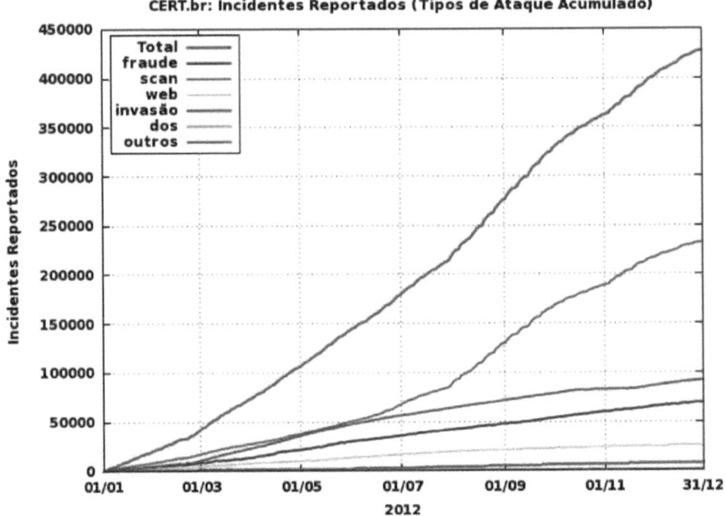

Figure 2 - Incidents reported to CERT.br
Source: CGI.br (2012)

In this new scenario, where the Information Society is increasingly active, there is a growing range of new equipment, such as mobile devices, new possibilities for using and storing information on the web (social networks, cloud computing, etc.). These devices and services handle both personal and corporate information and therefore require attention to protect. According to Marcelo Bechara (2010), in 2009 the use of corporate mobile phones as a work tool was a reality in 65% of companies that have computers. Of this percentage, only a quarter (%) use corporate mobile phones to access the Internet; while 45% of the same universe use SMS and MMS messaging, and 25% send and receive emails via mobile terminals. Considering the total number of companies that use the Internet, 10% in 2009 did so via a 3G mobile/modem connection, a 100% increase on the previous year.

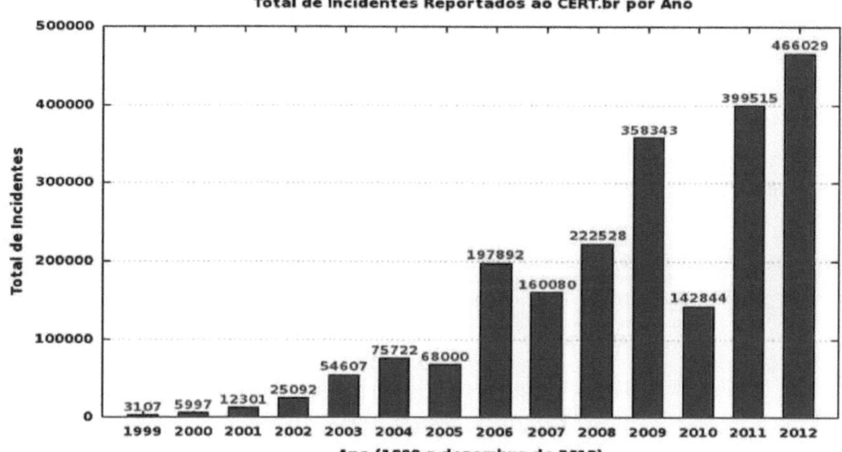

Figure 3 - Total Incidents Reported to CERT.br per Year
Source: CERT.br (2013)

Figure 3 shows the increasing frequency of total incidents reported to CERT.br by Brazilian companies and institutions between 1999 and 2012. It is worth highlighting the year 2010, when there was a drop. According to Cristine Hoepers, security analyst at CERT.br:

> [...] the reduction in notifications of attempted fraud, which led to the fall in the 2010 total, is related to the fall in notifications of possible copyright infringements through the distribution of material on P2P networks.(CERT.br, 2011, p. 39)

Information is crucial to the Federal Public Administration (FPA), but it is also exposed to major risks. The pillars of information security, which are availability, integrity, confidentiality and authenticity, are subject to vulnerabilities (MANDARINO JÚNIOR E CANONGIA, 2010).

This environment, which includes vulnerabilities, attacks and devices containing important information and providing diverse access to corporate and government networks, requires careful attention from the authorities responsible for how information and services are accessed and delivered to the end user. Pinheiro (2009) presents a list of the greatest vulnerabilities observed in cyber environments:

- Dependence on external systems and technologies;

- Low investment in research and development in research centres and universities, especially in Information Security;

- Obsolete or foreign telecommunications and energy infrastructure;

- Low development and culture in Information Security in Institutions and Knowledge Protection;

- Low training of the judiciary in cyber-crime and electronic evidence;

- Legislation to respond to international requests for co-operation and national investigations.

- Allowing traceability;

- Lack of standardisation for incident response;

- Lack of an implemented Brazilian cyber security plan.

Lemos (2007) defines this scenario, known as cyberspace, as:

> Cyberspace is both a locus of territorialisation (mapping, control, search engines, agents, surveillance) and also of reterritorialisation (blogs, chats, P2P, mobile technologies). Socio-cultural disengagement and space-time compression create a mixture of dematerialisation and discontinuity. Deterritorialisation creates new forms of territorialisation that move social life and can act against the sclerosis of social institutions, destabilising the architectures of power (LEMOS, 2007, p. 23).

In 2009, US President Barack Obama gave a speech focused exclusively on his country's cyber security and referred to cyberspace as "[...] it's a world we depend on every day" (UNITED STATES OF AMERICA, 2009, p. 2). In this context of ever-increasing digital inclusion, the availability of public services on the Internet, which makes up cyberspace, is increasing. This requires greater control and management of the security of this environment.

Mandarino Junior and Canongia (2010) warn of the real need for Brazil to prepare for possible attacks that are already happening around the world. The lack of threats on Brazil's physical borders with neighbouring countries leads Brazilian society not to attach greater importance to national defence issues, but this reasoning cannot be applied to cyberspace. According to Endler (2001), it is important to emphasise that the Internet has become the main channel of communication between government and citizens. Relationships are now virtual and require special care with systems security.

With the visibility that Brazil has achieved on the world stage, the eyes of cyber criminals have turned to the country. According to Figure 4, which shows the number of incidents reported to CGI.br, it can be seen that in the last 10 years the number of attacks has increased by 1,757.28%. It should be noted that Brazil occupies a prominent position and that the Federal Government has shown concern for the defence of Brazil's borders, both physical in the National Defence Strategy and cyber, as we can see in Ordinance 45 of the Institutional Security Office, which set up the Cyber Security Technical Group:

> [...] the increase in threats and attempted cyber attacks, which include potential attacks on government networks and databases, affecting the Federal Public Administration;
> [...] the real possibility of using computational means for offensive actions against the computer networks of strategic institutions of the Brazilian Government, resolves and establishes:
> Art. 1º The Cyber Security Technical Group is hereby established with the aim of proposing guidelines and strategies for Cyber Security within the scope of the Federal Public Administration.

In the interview given by Mr Raphael Mandarino, Director of the Department of Information Security and Communications of the Presidency of the Republic of Brazil, it is possible to get an idea of the various attacks that the Brazilian Federal Government network receives and the vulnerability of our network infrastructure. He replied as follows:

> [...] Government networks receive 2,100 attacks an hour. I always give the figure for the previous year so as not to generate too much speculation. And 2,100 is actually 1% of the attacks we receive, but that 1% is the attack I can identify as the most serious. These are attempts to steal information, both from people in government and from government projects. Imagine a research company that has a project that hasn't yet been patented and that company receives an invasion attack to steal that project. These 2,100 attacks per hour are at that level. It's less than the United States, that's for sure. For example, the 60 Minutes programme recently made a statement that the blackout [the programme was talking about the 2005 and 2007 problems, but there were also suspicions about 2009] was caused by hackers. I refuted that statement by saying that a large part of our systems are not interconnected. The central command of the regulatory agency is made to command someone manually [the computer distributes orders that are executed by people]. In other words, there are people in the system, not machines]. Of course, part of the infrastructure is automated, and part is not. Causing a blackout of that proportion by means of an internet attack I would say is unlikely. (FAGUNDES, 2010, p. 2)

It's worth pointing out that in the Internet environment, these incidents and cyber-crimes have been happening for some time. In 2007, an attack in Estonia was publicised, and at the time it was considered "the biggest cyber-attack in history", as it made it impossible for Estonia to access the network.

> The internet war was an obvious form of retaliation against the Estonian government. The websites of the Presidency of the Republic, the Parliament, political parties and banks were hacked in order to post phrases and photos of Soviet soldiers. Even more serious was the use of viruses to overload Estonian servers and prevent them from working. To do this, hackers spread invader programmes on thousands of computers around the world which, with a simple command, clogged Estonian machines with junk mail, which crashed without being able to cope with the avalanche of information. As computers have an IP number to access the internet, it was possible to find out where the attacks came from. Most of them came from Russia and Russian government institutions. The Kremlin says that this doesn't prove anything, as IP numbers can be easily falsified. "The criminals could be anywhere, even in South Africa or Brazil," agrees Rogério de Campos Morais, director of IBM's security division in São Paulo (TEIXEIRA, 2007, p. 31).

Cyber attacks are on the increase worldwide and are a major challenge for governments. For this reason, Cyber Security and Cyber Defence are becoming increasingly important as strategic government functions:

- Protection of critical infrastructures;
- Information and communications security;
- International co-operation;
- Building legal frameworks;
- Training human resources.

Based on the above, there is no doubt about the importance of cyber security. This area has been impacted by the evolution and convergence of ICTs, due to the reduction in *hardware* and *software* costs, the increased availability of systems and networks and the universalisation of internet access.

1.1 PROBLEMATISATION

The facts set out in the introduction to this work seek to demonstrate the consequences of the emergence of cyberspace, the constantly and rapidly changing habits and customs and the increase in threats and vulnerabilities. What all this does is force states to create a culture of Information and Communication Security (CIS). This situation influences the development of a culture in the area of Information and Communication Security (CIS) and the role of the state in promoting cyber security and defence.

In 2008, Decree No.[0] 6.703 of 18 December 2008 was published by the President of the Republic, at the time Luis Inácio Lula da Silva, which approved the National Defence Strategy (END), stating that it was necessary to take measures to secure critical infrastructure areas, including services, especially with regard to energy, transport, water and telecommunications, in charge of the Ministries of Defence, Mines and Energy, Transport, National Integration and Communications, water and telecommunications, which is the responsibility of the Ministries of Defence, Mines and Energy, Transport, National Integration and Communications, and the work of coordination, evaluation, monitoring and risk reduction was assigned to the Office of Institutional Security of the Presidency of the Republic (GSI/PR) (BRASIL, 2008). The Decree also states that the Commander of the Army is responsible for implementing the END and will formulate its cyber defence policy and doctrine and prepare its operational and support bodies to fulfil its constitutional purpose.

After the launch of the END in 2012, the Cyber Defence Policy (PCD) was created, which includes guidelines for the application and development of actions in all components of the military expression of National Power, as well as in entities that may participate in Defence or Cyber Warfare activities (BRASIL, 2012). In addition, the PCD creates the Military Cyber Defence System (SMDC) in the Armed Forces, with the power to crack down on cybercrime. The SMDC will include the participation of military, civilian and academic personnel; it must also jointly ensure the effective use of cyberspace (preparation and operational use) by the Armed Forces; and prevent or hinder its use. The PCD also establishes the creation of an incident response team, which will carry out war exercises and simulated attacks.

However, the policy document does not address some aspects that are fundamental to the constitution of international cooperation, i.e. strategic alliances for the contributions and growth of the allied parties. For example, the security policies of the USA (2009), the Republic of South Africa (2011) and India (2011) contain guidelines and actions related to international cooperation to promote global coordination of responses to threats and vulnerabilities, participation in events to level knowledge and the creation of bilateral and/or multilateral partnerships for coordinated actions. It can thus be seen that there are different guidelines between the cyber security policies of different countries, despite the fact that the problems and vulnerabilities in this area are common knowledge. This may be expected for some specific guidelines, but it is doubtful for issues of the same nature and of great relevance. Therefore, given the importance of the issue for national security and sovereignty, this research question arises: **which cyber security policy guidelines need attention from the Brazilian authorities, based on the knowledge of other countries in the area?**

1.2   GENERAL AND SPECIFIC OBJECTIVES

1.2.1   GENERAL OBJECTIVE

Evaluate Brazil's Cyber Defence Policy (PCD) to see if it adheres to the policies of other countries, with a view to enriching the discussion of future actions for the defence of Brazilian cyberspace.

1.2.2   SPECIFIC OBJECTIVES

- Analysing the cyber security policies of other countries;
- Identify the main guidelines and aspects of the policies analysed;
- Evaluate the PCD, based on an analysis of other countries' policies;
- Check the relevance of the results of the analysis with experts in the field;
- Characterise the relevant aspects that need attention for the adoption of PCD.

1.3   BACKGROUND

Observing the exponential growth in the total number of incidents reported to CERT.br (2012) per year, it is understood that there is an urgent need for security measures that make it difficult to divert information and make the country's critical infrastructure services unavailable. The current level of concern regarding cyberspace by all nations is remarkable. According to Espindula (2012), the Brazilian government should adopt all necessary measures to monitor and advise on cyber threat mitigation, and coordinate the national response to any cybersecurity incident.

It is understood that Brazil should step up its actions in this area. It is worth mentioning that Brazil has not ratified the Council of Europe Convention on Cybercrime, and has not even implemented legislation to ratify this treaty (ESPINDULA, 2012). The author believes that it is inevitable to support international efforts to develop and implement a global cyber governance regime to improve our internal and external security, in order to help build the cyber security capacity of less developed states and foreign partners. These measures can help prevent adversaries from exploiting weak links in global cyber defence.

There is a limited role for communication bodies in the governance structure of cyber security in Brazil. According to Alves Júnior (2011), few concrete activities (beyond the ideological level) have been identified in the Brazilian case, nor has the inclusion of agencies or ministries in the central activity of formulating cyber security policies. On the other hand, the GSI has produced material, held events, trained manpower and stimulated the participation of the specialised community.

According to Cruz (2012), the domain of cyberspace is a major challenge in this century, becoming a new frontier to be explored due to its unprecedented nature and asymmetry. The novelty is due to the lack of models and references, as well as the absence of legal frameworks. Asymmetry is related to the difference in power, where the strongest can have an advantage, i.e. be ahead of other countries in terms of the security of their cyberspace.

According to Espindula (2012), Brazil's defence strategy and cyber defence policy were created around the concept of "independence". In the government's view, Brazil should be able to control its own security and should not need to look outside its borders for the instruments of its security forces. The strategy envisages the existence of strategic partners, but these are seen as countries willing to transfer technologies to Brazil that make Brazil more independent, rather than as collaborators in security operations.

Cyber security policies are indispensable for carrying out actions and strengthening governance in this area. Cyberspace and critical infrastructure are strategic in nature, as they play an essential role in national sovereignty, cultural integration and economic development. For this reason, protecting them must be a permanent strategic objective, in order to ensure the continued operation of essential services.

Bezerra (2012) describes the different views on decision-making and policies in some countries in the current cyber context.

> Fortunately, the Brazilian government is also organising itself, with the Department of Information and Communications Security (DSIC), which is part of the Office of Institutional Security of the Presidency of the Republic, which is a good sign, as it reports directly to the President. A centralised coordination and planning structure is really essential. [...]
> Compared to its counterparts in North America and Great Britain, the DSIC today has more prosaic but no less complex challenges: disseminating information security concepts to almost a million civil servants. That doesn't mean it's any less important. [On the other hand, the Brazilian government has some of the best and best prepared attack response groups in the country, in companies such as Banco do Brasil, Petrobras and Serpro. Gradually this knowledge will be disseminated to state and municipal governments, as well as private companies.
> We don't need to go as far as Pakistan, which proclaimed a law in 2008 that punishes the perpetrators of cyber-terrorism with the death penalty, but it is essential that digital infrastructure and services, as well as sensitive and important data for the country, are protected (BEZERRA, 2012, p. 2).

A preliminary assessment revealed that there are no studies on comparisons of cyber security policies, nor on the relevance of the guidelines that should be included in documents of this nature. On the other hand, there have been studies that indicate specific problems apparent in the policies in non-scientific analyses, such as Suffert (2012), who briefly compares the policies of Brazil and India. Given the lack of studies on the subject, this paper analyses the cyber security policies of Brazil and some other countries, making it possible to understand the degree of comprehensiveness of these policies and the approach used. In addition, it highlights the main cyber security policy guidelines analysed, thus enabling the identification of gaps and recurring themes that can be considered when designing, reviewing and implementing policies in this area.

CHAPTER 2

LITERATURE REVIEW

As humanity has evolved, territories have expanded their operating environments, such as land, water and space. We are now discussing a new operating environment, cyberspace, whose environment is located on the Internet. The term cyberspace was coined by Willian Gibson in his novel Neuromancer (APDSI, 2005). Cyberspace (or cyberspace) is considered to be the metaphor that describes the non-physical space created by computer networks, notably the internet, where people can communicate in different ways, through electronic messages, chat rooms, discussion groups, among others.

Cyberspace was described by Levy (1994), who used a vision of collective and mutating intelligence, based on exchanges of knowledge and networks, as follows:

> Cyberspace is a terrain where humanity is functioning today. [It is the establishment of a network of all computerised memories and all computers. [...] With cyberspace we have a communication tool that is very different from classic media, because it is in this space that all messages become interactive, gain plasticity and have the possibility of immediate metamorphosis. [...] Within cyberspace we find a variety of tools, devices and intellectual technologies. For example, one aspect that is developing more and more at the moment is artificial intelligence. There are also hypertexts, interactive multimedia, simulations, virtual worlds, telepresence devices (LEVY, 1994, p. 38).

More developed governments are more vulnerable because they depend on complex cyber systems, such as systems that manage nuclear, hydroelectric and aerospace power stations, military and economic actions. As such, Nye (2012) observes that cyberspace, as well as being a source of information resources and services, is also becoming a source of insecurity for rich countries.

This cyber space offers a range of services and its environment is home to sensitive information that is subject to daily threats due to its value and importance. Glenny (2011, p. 234) notes that "The first threat is cybercrime; the second, electronic industrial espionage; and the third, *cyberwar*". Symantec, a company specialising in computer security, data protection and remote management software, defines the term cybercrime as any crime in which a computer, network or *hardware* device has been used (2012 NORTON STUDY, 2012).

Two actors who are always present across the threat spectrum are the spy and the *hacker*. The *hacker,* according to Crespo (2011, p. 95), is the generic name given to so-called computer pirates. This expression originated in the computer labs of the *Massachusetts Institute of Technology* (MIT), where students would spend sleepless nights analysing everything that could be done with a computer. And the concept of spy, according to Moreira (1999), refers to a person who illegally intercepts communications.

Moresi (2011) explains that cyber security has been one of the major challenges facing the governments of various countries, particularly in terms of guaranteeing the functioning of critical infrastructures such as energy, defence, transport, telecommunications, finance and others. The terms *cyberdefence, cybersecurity* and *cyberwar* are similar, but at the same time they have different concepts, which is why it is important to distinguish the differences between them.

We can describe the term cyber warfare as a tool for political or military action. Digital crime expert Milagre (2012) defines cyber warfare in three different ways. According to the development of the conflict, according to the type of weapon and according to the forces employed in the confrontation:

> *Cyberwar* according to the development of the conflict: cold war (indirect, espionage, subversion or technological conflicts) or subversive or guerrilla warfare (unconventional warfare, the aim of which is to subvert the established order) - It can also be classified as psychological warfare;
> Cyberwar by type of weapon: technological warfare;
> Cyberwar according to the opposing forces: irregular warfare, fought between an army and a guerrilla group, with an undefined battlefield. It is difficult to distinguish between civilians and soldiers. But it can also be regular, between virtual armies; (MILAGRE, 2012, p. 3).

For Mandarino Junior and Canongia (2010), the difference between cyber security and cyber defence is that the first term encompasses aspects and attitudes of both prevention and repression, and the second term covers operational actions of offensive combat.

According to Campen (1996), cyber security is the offensive and defensive use of information and information systems to deny, exploit, corrupt or destroy the adversary's values, based on information, information systems and computer networks. Actions can be designed to gain advantages in military, civilian and asymmetric warfare due to their low-cost feasibility and high impact. According to Lind (2005), the meaning of asymmetric warfare is

> War in which the opponents have various differences, such as: level of organisation, objectives, financial resources, military resources, behaviour - obedience to rules. They are generally irregular wars (guerrilla wars), insurrectionary wars or wars between powers and small states. The actions of the weaker party are generally indirect and aimed at wearing down the stronger party. When there is victory, it is usually not military, but is achieved by the military and political attrition of one of the combatants, to a degree that leads to them giving up fighting. (LIND, 2005, p. 2)

According to the *Department of Homeland Security*'s National Infrastructure *Protection Plan* (2009, p. 37), the term cyber security refers to

> [...] prevention of damage caused by unauthorised use of electronic information and communications systems and the information contained therein, with a view to ensuring confidentiality, integrity and availability, including actions to restore electronic information and communications systems in the event of a terrorist attack or natural disaster.

The definition of cyber security used by the Federal Government is that of Ordinance No. 45 (BRASIL, 2009) *in verbis*:

> Art. 2° Cybersecurity is considered to be the art (sic) of ensuring the existence and continuity of a nation's Information Society by guaranteeing and protecting its Information Assets and Critical Infrastructures in Cyberspace. (BRASIL, 2009, p. 2)

Also according to Ordinance 45 (BRASIL, 2009), the public sphere uses two terms aligned with the notion of cyber security: (i) critical information infrastructure; (ii) and information assets. In this document, critical information infrastructure is considered to be the subset of information assets that directly affect the fulfilment and continuity of the state's mission and the security of society. The concept of information assets, in turn, refers to the means of storing, transmitting and processing information, information systems, as well as the places where these means are located and the people who have access to them.

According to Salomão (2010), issues related to cyber security, to a large extent, both in terms of technology and in terms of guidelines, standardisation, methodologies and training, have been dealt with worldwide over the last few years within the scope of information and communications security, including in Brazil. However, the global picture shows that developed economies are currently reviewing or launching their national cyber security strategies, such as the US, UK, Japan, Spain, Australia and others. Issues of protecting countries' critical infrastructures are also being discussed, with a strong indication of how much remains to be done.

Mandarino Junior and Canongia (2009) studied the cyber security scenario in the United States of America and the United Kingdom. The authors discuss the launch of these countries' national security strategy plans and show that there is much to be done in the areas of international cooperation, legislation, standardisation and the training of specialised human resources.

To illustrate this, Annex 1 presents the framework of US and UK recommendations for the adopted National Cyber Security Strategy. The main differences between the countries are (MANDARINO JUNIOR and CANONGIA, 2009): (i) the UK is committed to creating a strategic alignment with international partners to exchange information and reference documents, in order to obtain a theoretical framework, best practices and required change initiatives; (ii) meanwhile, the US is committed to creating a body/agency to coordinate research and development in cyber. On the other hand, both countries are reinforcing the creation of a national security strategy, aimed at joint coordination in priority areas to establish an intra-government and inter-government programme.

CHAPTER 3

THEORETICAL FRAMEWORK

The literature review showed that the levels of cyber security that countries can adopt are:

- the national defence **strategy**: this is the operationalisation in which the processes are implemented;
- the cyber security **policy**: it covers rules of action and guidelines that must be applied; and
- the cyber security **model**: this comprises the planning, strategy and decision-making processes that will underpin governance.

This chapter will cover specific sections for each of these items, which represent different levels of security, and their importance in the current scenario.

3.1 NATIONAL DEFENCE STRATEGY

There is a great deal of effort being made in a scenario where there are many uncertainties about the development and conduct of national strategies for cyber security policies. The exchange of information and international experiences is a basic premise. Once the various countries are connected, it is likely that the nations' considerations and interests will coincide and converge on common aspects. This is also a choice that depends on the strategic alliances formed, according to each country's foreign policy.

According to Brasil (2008, p. 5), the concept of the National Defence Strategy (END) encompasses the concept of cyber security, a sector that must be protected by the government:

> The National Defence Strategy is the **link between the concept and policy of** national independence, on the one hand, and the Armed Forces to safeguard that independence, on the other. It deals with political and institutional issues that are decisive for the country's defence, such as the objectives of its "grand strategy" and the means to get the nation to participate in defence. It also addresses properly military problems, derived from the influence of this 'grand strategy' on the orientation and **operational practices of** the three Forces. The National Defence Strategy will be complemented by plans for peace and war, designed to deal with different employment scenarios.

According to Alves Júnior (2011), the United States already has a certain tradition of formulating cyber security strategies. Both Bill Clinton's administration in 2000 and George W. Bush's in 2002 and 2008 drew up programmes with this motto.

Lewis (2008) reports that the Cyber Security Commission of *Centrefor Strategic & International Studies* (CSIS) has the task of protecting cyberspace in the Presidency of the United Nations.

United States, and help guide policy formulation. The new US administration has cyber security on its agenda and is making a serious effort to understand what has already been achieved in the area and improve its national cyber posture. But there is much to be done. Constituting cybersecurity will be a long-term endeavour and hard work (LEWIS, 2008).

Baker (2013) points out that Australia has set up a new National Cyber Security Operations Centre, with a focus on operational capacity and the possibility of direct execution. This body is more focused on national defence strategy than politics and works together with owners and operators of critical infrastructure. In the US, on the other hand, the agencies have decided on an approach based on guidelines and actions, concentrating their efforts on information security policy. The Russian government, on the other hand, has opted for a more informal approach (BAKER, 2013). In that country, although there is no national cyber exercise plan and little institutional provision for partnerships or information sharing, government agents "have very close relationships with Internet service providers and within the providers there are people who are aware of the network situation in real time" and who keep them informed.

In Brazil, according to Mandarino Junior and Canongia (2010), the document Livro Verde: Segurança Cibernética no Brasil (Green Book: Cyber Security in Brazil), which is a mere government report with non-binding proposals, had the objective, at the time of its publication in 2010, of modifying or drafting a law on the subject. It also sought to encourage specialists in the area to contribute to the discussion, with a view to drawing up a possible cyber security policy. In other words, although the country did not have an established policy, there was a concern that it should be developed.

In addition, according to the aforementioned authors, a Technical Group was set up, made up of the following bodies: GSI, Ministry of Justice, Ministry of Defence, Ministry of Foreign Affairs, Navy Command, Army Command and Aeronautics Command, with the aim of proposing guidelines and strategies for cyber security, within the scope of the Federal Public Administration.

According to Bertonha (2009), the need for greater integration of civilians into the military system (and vice versa) is another point to be highlighted in the composition of a cyber defence strategy. This orientation clearly indicates the need for civilians to assume their role as the ultimate definers of defence issues and the subordination of the military to civilian powers. In addition, the author noted in the END that the situation of the Brazilian armed forces is also essentially correct: precarious and technologically outdated equipment, concentration of troops in less strategically sensitive areas, poor coordination between the various forces, purchases based on opportunities rather than needs, a deficient mobilisation system, an almost non-existent military industrial complex and dependence on foreign countries for sensitive equipment and technologies.

Despite the efforts made by the Brazilian Armed Forces, technological dependence on other nations is certainly a major problem, because in a real war situation this relationship of submission could be used by the enemy to affect Brazil. It should be noted that technological independence is a powerful weapon, especially cybernetic, to stand out at a critical moment like the one described above.

3.2 CYBER SECURITY POLICY

According to Hunker (2010), a cyber security policy refers to the measures taken to ensure security in cyberspace. Not only government agencies should build such measures, but private companies, internet providers and NGOs should adopt cyber security policies. According to Hunker (2010), the first thought evoked by cyber security policy is protection against cybercrime. However, policies are also based on infrastructures linked to cyberspace and data storage and exchange made by individuals, companies and government agencies based on the culture and peculiarities of each country that creates them.

According to Brasil (2012), the cyber security policy "aims to guide, within the Ministry of Defence (MD), the activities of Cyber Defence, at the strategic level, and Cyber Warfare, **at the operational and tactical levels, in** order to achieve its objectives". The objectives presented in Brasil (2012) are:

> The objectives of the Cyber Defence Policy are:
> a)   jointly ensuring the effective use of cyberspace (preparation and operational use) by the Armed Forces (AF) and preventing or hindering its use against the interests of National Defence; or hindering its use against the interests of National Defence;
> b)   to train and manage the human talent needed to conduct the activities of the Cyber Sector (St Cyber) within the MD;
> c)   collaborate in the production of intelligence knowledge from cyber sources of interest to the Defence Intelligence System (SINDE) and to government bodies involved in CIS and Cyber Security, in particular the Office of Institutional Security of the Presidency of the Republic (GSI/PR);
> d)   develop and keep up-to-date the doctrine for the use of St Cyber;
> e)   implement measures that contribute to SIC Management within the MD;
> f)   adapting the S,T&I structures of the three Forces and implementing research and development activities to meet the needs of St Cyber;
> g)   define the basic principles that will guide the creation of specific legislation and standards for employment in St Cyber;
> h)   cooperate with the national and military mobilisation effort to ensure the operational capacity and, consequently, the deterrent capacity of St Cyber; and
> i)   contribute to the security of the information assets of the Federal Public Administration (FPA), with regard to Cyber Security, located outside the scope of the MD. (BRASIL, 2012, p. 2)

In relation to Brazilian cyberspace, Hosang (2011) reports that this environment, in general, does not have efficient security due to the following aspects:

- There is no standardised taxonomy on the subject, and most of the definitions are imported or not supported by Brazilian legislation, or even out of date.
- the lack of definition of the Brazilian state on the subject in relation to other countries; and
- there is no definition of a brazilian state body that can coordinate/articulate policies and activities related to cyber security at a national level.

The author also clarifies that the National Cyber Security Policy (PNSC) solves the challenge of forming common sense so that the country can grow securely, appropriating the benefits of the internet, a global network in continuous change, minimising negative impacts resulting from any disasters or malicious use to affect Brazil's critical infrastructure systems.

Strategy has a strong relationship with policy, because according to Ribeiro (2011), the scope of a strategic direction includes the creation of a specialised reference centre, the development of methodologies and systems, the definition of metrics and indicators and cooperation between the public and private sectors, as well as the international community. These elements must be based on a legal framework and regulatory framework that are consistent with these goals, based on a cyber security policy.

The Cyber Defence Policy (PCD) applies to all components of the military expression of

National Power, as well as to entities that may participate in Defence or Cyber Warfare activities (BRASIL, 2012). The PCD's main objectives are:

- jointly ensuring the effective use of cyberspace (preparation and operational use) by the Armed Forces (AF) and preventing or hindering its use against the interests of National Defence;
- to train and manage the human talent needed to conduct the activities of the Cyber Sector;
- collaborate with the production of intelligence knowledge;
- define the basic principles that will guide the creation of specific legislation and standards for employment in the cyber sector;
- contribute to the security of the information assets of the Federal Public Administration (FPA), with regard to Cyber Security, located outside the scope of the MD.

It can be seen that the countries' security policy approaches are different. However, it was not possible to identify in the literature a detailed comparative analysis of cyber security policies between countries, which is one of the aims of this work. The exception is the study by Alves Júnior (2011), who researched the security policies of the USA, the ITU and Brazil's situation in this area. The author introduces a blueprint for the future of cyber security in Brazil and interprets the recommendations of the Organisation for Economic Co-operation and Development (OECD), originally designed to indicate essential competences for the protection of critical infrastructures, as follows (ALVES JÚNIOR, 2011):

- define policy and specific rules, with clear objectives, at the highest level of government;
- promoting a culture of cyber security;
- promote mutual co-operation between *slakeholders*;
- act transparently;
- systematically review policy, standards and legal frameworks;
- closer relations with the private sector, through PPPs; and
- stimulate innovation through research and development.

Despite the lack of studies in the area, some aspects of differentiation between the policies can be seen. In the US policy alone (2009), the actors involved are allied countries, the civilian population, public and private companies and government entities. These actors are involved in both the development of cyber security policy and defence. The US concern is to develop US government positions for an international cyber security framework and policy, strengthening international partnerships to create initiatives that address the full range of activities, policies and opportunities associated with cyber security. The policy of the Republic of South Africa (2011), on the other hand, includes allied countries and allows for the participation of stakeholder groups, especially in the development and updating of its policy. And in India's policy (2011), the target audience refers to all

ICT users and suppliers, including civilians, small, medium and large companies and governmental and non-governmental organisations. In Brazil, the PCD does not specify the actors directly involved in the composition of cyber security groups in Brazil. It only mentions that it will have the collaboration of military personnel from the Armed Forces and civilians.

In order to promote the production of intelligence knowledge, the relevant information and communication security bodies will be integrated to create the: Military Cyber Defence System (SMDC). With this measure, the objectives of training and managing human talent; collaborating in the production of intelligence knowledge; and developing and keeping the policy up to date will become more homogeneous (BRASIL, 2012). Concerns about the creation of an incident response team are noted in India (2001), as each organisation in the country's critical sector must have a team that will be part of their respective bodies/agencies.

Some items recur in all the policies mentioned in this chapter and the most important are:

- creation of a cyber security coordination centre;
- creation of an incident response team;
- concern for training, development and research;
- promoting and strengthening local co-operation; and
- acquisition of own or acquired cryptography.

As we saw earlier, the national defence strategy is related to the cyber security policy in a complementary relationship, in which actions are guided at the operational and tactical level in accordance with the guidelines. For these documents to remain up to date, it is essential to promote and guarantee the viability and maintenance in the short, medium and long term of actions related to providing security to critical infrastructures. In this way, the END and the PCD are also dependent on the model, which will act as a guideline and facilitator for the country's cyber security governance.

Looking at policies and strategies, it can be concluded that the cyber security model must encompass the formulation, implementation, control and review of policies, guidelines, rules, procedures, instruments and technologies that guide the practice of managing this model. For the model to be solid, it is important that the cyber security policy considers all the security gaps and, above all, the participation of the indispensable actors in its planning, execution, verification and action.

3.3 CYBER SECURITY MODELS

As mentioned, the END and the PCD establish the levels of operationalisation and the guidelines related to cyber security. According to Brasil (2012), the next challenge is to draw up a document that includes the requirements and elements of governance, with topics related to integrated planning, strategy and decision-making. This document is called the Cyber Security Model.

At the National Computer Science Research Meeting, Mandarino Junior and Canongia (2011) discuss their study on Brazil in terms of information - with the focus on cyber security as a challenge to national security - and conclude that there is no formatted and tested model for formalising structured actions to prevent and combat cyber attacks and crimes. It is worth noting that the Federal Government published Ordinance No. 45 of 21 December 2012 in the Federal Official Gazette, which created the Cyber Security Technical Group, made up of representatives from the Ministries of Justice, Defence, Foreign Affairs and the Commanders of the Armed Forces (BRASIL, 2012).

The Federal Public Administration shows real commitment and caution in creating a cyber security model to protect cyberspace and the services and information that exist in it, thus adapting to the current cyber crime scenario (PRESIDÊNCIA DA REPÚBLICA, 2010, p.17). This technical group began its work with the aim of:

[...] express potential strategic guidelines for the establishment of the National Cyber Security Policy, articulating a short (2 to 3 years), medium (5 to 7 years), and long (10 to 15 years) term vision on the subject, covering, as a starting point, the following vectors: Political-Strategic, Economic, Social and Environmental, ST&I, Education, Legal, International Cooperation, and Critical Infrastructure Security. (PRESIDÊNCIA DA REPÚBLICA, 2010, p.17)

It can be said that there are already several efforts to create cyber security models. A good example, cited in the scientific journal *NetworkSecurity* (2009), is the US Department of Energy scientists at *Argonne National Laboratory*, who have developed a model called the Federal Model for Cyber Security to defend against attacks. The idea is that cyber security defence systems can continue to communicate, even when an attack, such as DDoS, is in progress.

According to *NetWork Security* (2009) "The Federal Model for Cyber Security acts as a virtual programme. If an institution suffers an attack on its infrastructure, secure and timely communication with the other agencies of the Federation will help protect it from the attack and even through active response." In its current state, the system transmits information about suspicious IP addresses and domain names, but will soon be able to share suspicious email addresses and web URLs between Federation systems. The development of the system won the *DoE 2009 Cyber Security Innovation Achievement Award*. As well as protecting government assets, the team believes it can be used in the private sector.

In addition, NIST (2013), the *National Institute of Standards and Technology,* which recognises that US national and economic security depends on the reliable operation of critical infrastructure, was appointed by the President of the United States to develop a voluntary model to reduce cyber risks to critical infrastructure in conjunction with stakeholders. The model will consist of standards, guidelines and best practices and aims to promote the protection of information and information systems supporting critical infrastructure operations. This model will help managers and operators of critical infrastructure to manage cyber security and risks related to commercial confidentiality, individual privacy and civil liberties.

To develop the model, NIST (2013) will collect information on the capabilities of various suppliers to:

- identify existing cyber security standards, guidelines, frameworks and best practices applicable to the security of critical infrastructure sectors and other stakeholders;
- specify high priority in identifying gaps for which standards (new or revised) are needed, and
- collaboratively develop action plans to resolve the gaps identified.

Models are important for the development and understanding of cyber security theory. These models can support and predict risks. In this case, models can predict attack risks and their impacts (BAKER, 2012, p. 36).

Finally, according to Baker (2013), the absence of a cyber security model can lead to conflicts of jurisdiction on this issue. Kimberly Zenz (apud BAKER, 2012, p. 30) gives some examples of this situation:

> There is a lot of infighting in Russian government bodies. There are disputes at all levels. All the federal organisations, even within the same ministry, are fighting each other." In the United States, friction in the executive branch is duplicated and amplified by conflicts between oversight committees in Congress. "Capitol Hill understands absolutely nothing about America's cybersecurity problems." (BAKER, 2013, p. 30)

CHAPTER 4

METHODOLOGY

In order to achieve the objectives of this study, this section presents the methodology used to carry out the research. Research methodology, as quoted below, means choosing systematic procedures for describing and explaining phenomena. These procedures are similar to those followed by the scientific method, which consists of defining a problem, making observations and interpreting them on the basis of the relationships found, based, if possible, on existing theories (RICHARDSON, 1985, p. 29).

Another view of the methodology is defined as follows:

> It consists of studying and evaluating the various methods available, identifying their limitations or not in terms of the implications of their use. Methodology, at an applied level, examines and evaluates research techniques as well as the generation or verification of new methods that lead to the capture and processing of information with a view to solving research problems (BARROS, 1986, p. 31).

4.1   RESEARCH CLASSIFICATION

According to Gil (2008), research is defined as the formal and systematic process of developing the scientific method. The fundamental aim of research is to find answers to problems through the use of scientific procedures. Based on this author's classification of research, this study can be characterised as:

- **From the point of view of its nature**, research is applied, as it aims to generate knowledge for practical applications aimed at solving specific problems;
- **From the point of view of the approach to the problem**, the research is qualitative, since there is a relationship that cannot be translated into numbers;
- **From the point of view of the objectives**, the research is exploratory, because it evaluates the existing guidelines in cyber security policies and presents the gaps that exist in the PCD;
- **From the point of view of technical procedures**, the techniques of content analysis and semi-structured interviews were chosen. Content analysis makes it possible, by categorising and organising the information contained in cyber security policy documents, to analyse Brazil's cyber defence policy in order to verify its adherence to the policies of other countries. Semi-structured interviews, in turn, make it possible to verify and evaluate the results found in the research with professionals in the sector.

4.2   CONTENT ANALYSIS

As already mentioned, this study analysed the cyber security policies of other countries in order to identify and assess relevant aspects of PCD. Content analysis, a qualitative data analysis technique, was used to analyse these policies. According to Bardin (1977, p. 42), content analysis comprises:

> [...] a set of techniques for analysing communications, aiming to obtain,

by systematic and objective procedures for describing the content of messages, indicators (quantitative or not) that allow the inference of knowledge related to the conditions of production/reception (inferred variables) of these messages.

Bardin (2011) presents the possible techniques used in content analysis: **categorical analysis**, evaluation analysis, enunciation analysis, expression analysis, relationship analysis and discourse analysis. The technique chosen for this study was categorical analysis, as it is an effective way of analysing discourse and works by breaking down the text into categories. When you discover a theme in the data, you have to compare statements and actions with each other to see if there is a concept that unifies them.

According to Bardin (2011), the technique of content analysis makes it possible to observe obscure messages that require interpretation, messages with a double meaning whose profound significance can only emerge after careful observation or a charismatic intuition. The technique is organised into three stages: pre-analysis, exploration of the material and treatment of the results.

4.2.1   PRE-ANALYSIS

In the pre-analysis stage, the following sequence was carried out:

- organising the material;
- choice of documents to be analysed;
- guiding questions;
- developing indicators to support the final interpretation.

The cyber security policies of the USA, UK, South Africa, India and Brazil were selected for analysis. Firstly, a floating reading was carried out, which highlighted some guiding questions, based on the known bibliography. The next step was to look at the policy guidelines related to the guiding questions. The themes that recurred very frequently were identified as candidates for the phase of selecting categories for thematic analysis, coding and recording the data.

4.2.2   EXPLORING THE MATERIAL

This stage is coding, in which the raw data is organised and aggregated into themes, in which the recording unit, counting rule and categories are also defined. According to Bardin (2011), the recording unit is the unit of meaning to be coded; it can be a theme, word or phrase.

The counting rule refers to the way in which the presence or absence of the recording elements is verified. In this study, frequency was used as the measure for counting the appearance of the recording unit. The recording unit chosen for its degree of relevance is: **policy guidelines**. The text segments are selected according to the recording unit. The choice of this recording unit was based on the content of the documents, specifically the aspects of interest to the study, i.e. identifying the main guidelines and aspects of the policies analysed in order to make a comparison with Brazil's PCD.

The definition of the categories made it possible to group the cybersecurity policy guidelines using the semantic classification criterion (themes and phrases). According to Bardin (2011), semantic categorisation is the grouping of elements (recording units) under a general heading based on common characteristics. Categories reflect reality and are syntheses of knowledge at a given moment. They are therefore constantly changing, just like reality. The procedure adopted for analysing the study is organised around categories.

4.2.3 PROCESSING THE RESULTS

According to Bardin (2011), the processing of the results comprises inference and interpretation. The latter stage consists of simple statistical treatment of the results, allowing tables to be drawn up that condense and highlight the information provided for analysis. Comparisons were made between the different themes to find similarities between them, and those that were similar were aggregated.

After processing the results, inference was made for subsequent verification by experts in the field, seeking to build scientific knowledge about the object being researched. Inferences lead to interpretations and in this last phase tables were drawn up for each of the questions, with the category and registration units. A simple statistical treatment was therefore used to interpret each of the questions.

4.2.4 SEMI-STRUCTURED INTERVIEW

According to Gil (2008), the interview is one of the most widely used data collection techniques in the social sciences. Psychologists, sociologists, pedagogues, social workers and practically all other professionals who deal with human problems use this technique, not only to collect data, but also for diagnostic and counselling purposes.

According to Tomar (2008), the semi-structured interview is closer to a conversation (dialogue) focused on certain subjects than a structured interview. It is based on an adaptable interview guide that is not rigid or predetermined.

Based on the methodological approach we used, the semi-structured interview seemed the most appropriate, since the interviewee was given some leeway to discuss the topic presented, with the aim of obtaining information about security policy guidelines that were completely unknown.

According to Grilo (2012), during the interview we tried to take advantage of some of the intrinsic advantages associated with this technique, such as: adaptability and flexibility; clarification of answers, complementation and testing; observation of the respondent's verbal and non-verbal behaviour; interaction with the interviewee to motivate them to answer. However, the difficulties and limitations of the technique were also taken into account: the high cost in time; the potential subjectivity; the interviewee's lack of freedom; the incorrect interpretation of the interviewee's statements; and the induction of the answer by the interviewer.

To carry out the interview, a script was drawn up beforehand, an attempt was made to establish an appropriate relationship with the interviewee on the basis of respect for them, the purpose of the interview was explained, authorisation was sought to audio-record the interview, anonymity was guaranteed, thanks were given for the interview and the interviewee was later given the text of the interview to make any corrections.

In order to interpret the information resulting from the interview, we proceeded with a content analysis, which is nothing more than a set of techniques for analysing communications, with the aim of obtaining, through systematic and objective procedures for describing the content of messages, quantitative indicators that allow the inference of knowledge relating to the conditions of production/reception of these messages (Bardin, 2011). To this end, we recorded the message data obtained with the help of categories that had been defined a priori but were enriched a posteriori.

In the interviews analysed, according to Bardin (2011), the categories were of the semantic type in which the theme was the most relevant recording unit. The semi-structured interviews were subject to thematic content analysis with the aim of extracting the meaning of the communication. This was an analysis at a semantic level that was not formalised but had the objectives of the interview as a backdrop.

CHAPTER 5

RESEARCH EXECUTION

Carrying out the research made it possible to understand the guidelines and, above all, the differences and similarities between the main cyber security policies analysed. Data collection was based on the policy documents, in this case in addition to comparing and discussing the differences and similarities between the guidelines contained in Brazil's Cyber Defence Policy and the policies investigated.

In order to achieve the aim of the study, the content of the published Cyber Security Policies of the USA, UK, South Africa and India was first analysed and then compared with the guidelines contained in the Brazilian CSP. As a second step, in order to clarify some of the results obtained and gather more information, a semi-structured interview was carried out due to its greater flexibility in exploring these issues.

5.1   CONTENT ANALYSIS

The content analysis began with the identification of the recording unit, and the one chosen was **policy guidelines** due to its importance to the study and its presence in all the documents analysed. As the documents are policies, which according to HOUAISS (2001) means the art or science of organising, directing and administering nations or states, the number of recording units was restricted to just one in this study.

According to Bardin (2011), each element can only exist in one category and if the categories are well defined and the indices and indicators that determine the entry of an element into a category are clear, there will be no distortions due to the subjectivity of the analysts.

With the registration unit chosen, we began to explore the material in order to determine the categories to house the guidelines analysed, so that we could compare them and see which converge and which diverge from Brazilian policy. The themes (indices) chosen according to the analysis of the guidelines were: **Information Security, Interaction with other bodies and actors, Cybersecurity Culture, Technical Cooperation, Security Infrastructure, Standardisation and Cybersecurity Training**. The following indicators were used to characterise the guideline in each category:

      - Information Security - Adaptation of cyber security structures and standards;

- **Interaction with other bodies and actors** - Interactions with APF bodies, local and international actors (individuals and organisations);

- **Cyber Security Culture** - Developing a cyber security culture;

- **Technical Co-operation** - Co-operation with actors to develop cyber security;

- **Security infrastructure** - Actions to improve cyber security;

- **Standardisation** - Development and adaptation of South African cyber security policies and standards;

- **Cybersecurity Training** - Training and mobilisation of specialised personnel.

With the scope of each category defined, we identified each of the policy guidelines under analysis and categorised them according to APPENDICES 1, 2, 3, 4 and 5, which are the cyber security policies of Brazil, South Africa, the United States of America, India and the United Kingdom, respectively. With the categorisation carried out, a code was created to identify all the policy guidelines under study and thus characterise each guideline analysed in Brazil's policy by pointing to the correlated guideline in the foreign country's policy.

In order to index the guidelines, coding and numbering were used to categorise them as follows:

- Firstly, the acronyms of the countries were given according to the international acronym standard, ISO3166;
- For Brazil the acronym is BR, for South Africa it's ZA, for the United States of America it's US, for India it's IN and for the United Kingdom it's GB;
- Each guideline was also numbered to help identify it.

Table 1 - Example of coding the guidelines analysed

ADHERENCE	CODE	GUIDELINES	CATEGORY
No Adherence	BR-42	Designing and implementing the military cyber defence system (SMDC), with the participation of AF military personnel and civilians;	Information Security
Partial Adherence	GB-79	Supporting the application of research, working with the Government Office for Science and others to build innovative cyber security solutions, drawing on our world-leading technical resources in support of our national security interests and wider economic prosperity.	Information Security
Non-adherence	BR-01	Identifying, registering and selecting staff with competences or skills, existing in the internal and external environments of the organisations, to join the SMDC;	Cybersecurity Training
Adherence	US-01	Expand support for key education and research and development programmes to ensure that the nation continues to have the capacity to compete in the information age economy.	Cybersecurity Training
Partial Adherence	IN-01	Identify members of management who have knowledge of the nature of the security problems and related information and designate them as your Point of Contact.	Cybersecurity Training
Adherence	GB-04	Promote the development of a cadre of qualified cyber security professionals so that the UK continues to maintain an edge in this area.	Cybersecurity Training
No Adherence	BR-08	Survey the critical information infrastructures associated with St Cyber to help build the situational awareness needed for cyber defence activities;	Technical Co-operation
Adherence	ZA-03	[NCSPF] Will provide for the establishment of collaboration with local stakeholders, and this collaboration will focus on: Inclusion of industry and creating an enabling environment for a successful partnership, Encouraging private sector groups with common security interests and collaborating with government including in the co-operation of industry groups, Bringing the private sector together with the public to hold forums and create a common sense of incident and vulnerability handling.	Technical co-operation
Adherence	US-03	Establish an Information and Communications Infrastructure Interagency Policy Committee (ICI-IPC), chaired by the National Security Council (NSC) and Homeland Security Council (HSC), as the primary policy coordination body for issues related to the realisation of a secure, reliable, and survivable global information and communications infrastructure and related capabilities.	Technical Co-operation
No Adherence	ZA-07	Participate in regional, African Union and international forums on issues pertaining to cyber security to ensure South Africa's foresight in defining and drawing up a global cyber security agenda to combat cyber crime and build secure and reliable information technology centres.	Cyber Security Culture
No Adherence	US-11	Signalling to the world that you are serious about tackling this challenge with strong leadership and vision	Cyber Security Culture
Adherence	IN-03	Enunciate the national information security policy and coordination in all aspects of information security governance in the country.	Cyber Security Culture
Adhesion GB-25	BR-23	Create cyber intelligence structures, as required by the central intelligence bodies of the FAs and the SMDC, to apply scientific	Security infrastructure

		and systematic methods, seeking to extract and analyse data from the cyber source, producing knowledge of interest;	
No Adherence	GB-21	Helping consumers respond to the cyber threats that will be the "new normal" by using social media to provide warnings about fraud or other online threats.	Security infrastructure

According to Table 1, the identification can be verified as follows: in the code field, item **IN-05** identifies the guideline **Creating a cybersecurity culture for responsible user behaviour and actions,** which it points to as the fifth guideline of India's cybersecurity policy. The category heading indicates which category the policy has been categorised according to the established criteria.

Once the process of categorising and identifying all the guidelines had been completed, it was noted that due to their objectivity, precision and clarity, there was no need to reclassify them, as Bardin (2011) points out.

This last stage consisted of processing the data in order to compare the policies of the foreign countries under study with the Brazilian policy. Firstly, the number of guidelines in each category of each policy was analysed. To do this, Bardin (2011) advises creating tables to help in this cycle of analysis. Table 2 shows the number of guidelines per category, so it is possible to get a preliminary view of some of the adherences to the categories, for example: In the US and Indian policies, there are no guidelines on security infrastructure. Brazil only focuses on extracting and analysing data from its security infrastructure for future knowledge production. Unlike the other foreign countries, South Africa and the United Kingdom are already looking at prioritising and adapting these infrastructures so that the ÁPF and the other actors involved in the actions can use these services safely.

Another point to note is Brazil's analysis of the category of cyber security training, which seeks coordination with teaching and research centres to increase the development of techniques, equipment and specialists in this sector, while South Africa does not address this category at all. When comparing the approach to cyber security training in the policies of the United States and India with that of Brazil, it can be seen that Brazilian policy emphasises actions that understand the importance of this approach for national development in the cyber sector.

Table 2 - Number of guidelines per category in the policies analysed

Categories	Number of Guidelines					Total by Category
	Brazil	South Africa	United States	India	United Kingdom	
Information Security	9	9	14	25	29	86
Interaction with other bodies and players	4	8	8	3	13	36
Cyber Security Culture	6	11	8	3	9	37
Technical Co-operation	9	4	5	0	5	23
Security infrastructure	1	5	0	0	5	11
Standardisation	14	9	9	4	12	48
Cybersecurity Training	7	0	2	2	6	17
Total	50	46	46	37	79	258

Once the categorisation was complete, an analysis was carried out of the guidelines contained in the policies under study that are in the same category, in order to verify the relationship between them. The guidelines were analysed between the Brazilian guidelines and those of the foreign country. The following attributes were analysed: total adherence, partial adherence, no adherence by the foreign country and Brazil or conflict in the guidelines. These attributes were characterised by the following assessments:

- Adherence: in order to establish total adherence between guidelines, it is necessary for both guidelines to have identical characteristics. For example, guideline BR-21 in the Brazilian PCD, categorised as 'Cyber Security Culture', details the following: Propose, to the federal government, the realisation of a national education campaign on cyber defence, aimed at national mobilisation, to raise the level of awareness of Brazilian society. The Indian guideline that is fully adhered to is IN-05 and states the following: Creating a cyber security culture for responsible user behaviour and actions.

- Partial adherence: in this attribute, the Brazilian policy guideline must have at least one characteristic that coincides with the foreign country's policy. For example, in the category of 'interaction with other bodies and actors', guideline BR-27 deals with the following action: Create a permanent committee, within the scope of defence, made up of representatives from the MD and invited guests from other ministries and development agencies, to intensify and explore new opportunities for cooperation in Science, Technology and Innovation, in areas of interest to the cyber sector. And the US directive states that: The President should consider appointing a cybersecurity policy officer in the White House, the report to the NSC and cumulate functions with the NEC, to coordinate cybersecurity related to the nation's policies and activities. This individual would chair the ICI-IPC and lead a robust process in consultation with other EOP elements to resolve competing priorities and coordinate interagency cybersecurity policy and strategy development. The relationship is partial because the Brazilian directive encourages the involvement of more actors such as guests from other ministries and representatives of the MD in this committee to explore opportunities for cooperation in Information Science and Technology at the national level.

- No adherence: to fit this attribute, the guidelines being analysed must not have any similar characteristics. For example, in the 'standardisation' category, an action described in Brazilian directive BR-30 that: Establish criteria and control the mobilisation and demobilisation of personnel for cyber defence activity, is not related to guidelines from the foreign country South Africa.

- Conflict in guidelines: when the characteristics of the guidelines under study differ from one another. In the study, there were no conflicting Brazilian guidelines compared to the guidelines of the foreign countries being analysed, as described in Table 3.

Now with the attributes stipulated, the relationship between the guidelines contained in

Brazil's PCD and those of one foreign country at a time contained in the same category was analysed. This was done for all the categories and countries analysed, as shown in Appendix 6.

As a result of this research, a comparative table was extracted with the number of guidelines listed by category, by the country that established them and the adherence data identified can be seen in Table 3.

Table 3 - Comparison of adherence between the guidelines in the policies analysed

Themes (Categories)		Adherence	Partial Adherence	No Adherence		Conflict in the Guidelines	Total Guidelines	
Information Security			Brazil	Foreign country	Brazil	Brazil	Foreign country	Brazil
Brazil	South Africa	4	0	6	5	0	9	9
Brazil	United States	7	0	9	2	0	15	
Brazil	india	5	1	19	3	0	25	
Brazil	United Kingdom	1	2	26	6	0	29	
Interaction with other bodies and players			Brazil	Foreign country	Brazil	Brazil	Foreign country	Brazil
Brazil	South Africa	4	0	6	0	0	8	4
Brazil	United States	2	1	4	1	0	8	
Brazil	india	3	0	1	1	0	3	
Brazil	United Kingdom	3	0	10	1	0	13	
Cyber Security Culture			Brazil	Foreign country	Brazil	Brazil	Foreign country	Brazil
Brazil	South Africa	4	0	4	2	0	11	6
Brazil	United States	3	1	3	2	0	7	
Brazil	india	3	0	0	3	0	3	
Brazil	United Kingdom	3	1	2	2	0	9	
Technical Co-operation			Brazil	Foreign country	Brazil	Brazil	Foreign country	Brazil
Brazil	South Africa	3	2	1	4	0	4	9
Brazil	United States	7	0	1	2	0	5	
Brazil	india	0	0	0	9	0	0	
Brazil	United Kingdom	0	1	4	8	0	5	
Security infrastructure			Brazil	Foreign country	Brazil	Brazil	Foreign country	Brazil
Brazil	South Africa	0	0	5	1	0	5	1
Brazil	United States	0	0	0	1	0	0	
Brazil	india	0	0	0	1	0	0	
Brazil	United Kingdom	1	0	5	0	0	6	
Standardisation			Brazil	Foreign country	Brazil	Brazil	Foreign country	Brazil
Brazil	South Africa	3	1	5	10	0	9	14
Brazil	United States	4	0	3	10	0	9	
Brazil	india	1	1	2	12	0	4	
Brazil	United Kingdom	3	1	9	10	0	12	
Cybersecurity Training			Brazil	Foreign country	Brazil	Brazil	Foreign country	Brazil
Brazil	South Africa	0	0	0	7	0	0	7
Brazil	United States	4	0	0	3	0	2	
Brazil	india	0	2	0	5	0	2	
Brazil	United Kingdom	2	0	3	5	0	6	

A preliminary analysis shows that the guidelines of the foreign countries are in line with those of the continents in Brazil's policy, and that there is no conflict between them, so it can be concluded that they all have the same approach. Given this initial scenario, a detailed assessment was then made of the guidelines belonging to the same categories, and to this end these guidelines were aggregated in graphs by category for better analysis.

In the first scenario presented in Figure 5, regarding the 'Information Security' category, there are two types of adherence between Brazil's guidelines and those of the United States and the United Kingdom. In relation to the US, there is strong adherence between the guidelines, unlike the UK guidelines. It can be seen that the UK guidelines, GB-54, GB-55, GB-56, GB-57 and GB-58, align actions to directly combat cyber-terrorism and, above all, cyber-crime, with the aim of guaranteeing the security of local actors such as industries and civilians in order to foster national development while respecting the individual's right to privacy. These points are not addressed by Brazil's PCD.

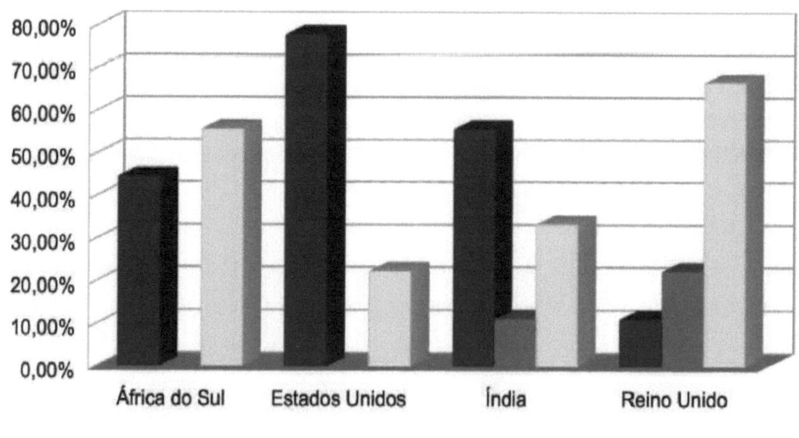

Figura 4 - Adherence to Information Security category guidelines

As seen in Figure 6, the Brazilian guidelines in the category of 'interaction with other bodies and actors' are fully in line with the South African guidelines in the same category. At this point, it can be seen that there is no more than 60% adherence to the US guidelines, because these guidelines do not address an action that Brazilian policy addresses in BR-25, which is the inclusion of cyber defence in combat simulation exercises and joint operations, bringing together other agencies of the APF to help national progress in the cyber defence sector.

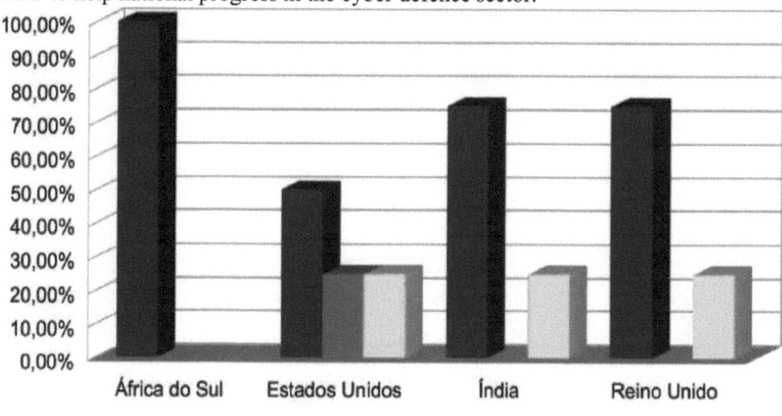

Figura 5 - Adherence to the guidelines of the Interaction with other bodies and actors category

Looking at Figure 7, it can be seen that it is in the 'cyber security culture' category that Brazilian policy adheres most closely to the policies of foreign countries. Some guidelines were not addressed in the Brazilian policy, but were addressed by the policies analysed, such as: Initiating national cybersecurity awareness campaigns; creating and maintaining situational awareness about risk in South African cyberspace, building a cybersecurity-based vision of identity management and strategy that addresses privacy in the interests of civil liberties, leveraging privacy-enhancing technologies for the nation and discussing what the nation can do to solve problems in a way that the American people can appreciate the need for action.

In the policies of foreign countries, it was found that the essence of the BR-20 guideline was not addressed and that in Brazil's policy, it was laid out as a guideline for identifying both individual and organisational competences, seeking partnerships with a view to exchanging experiences in the cyber sector.

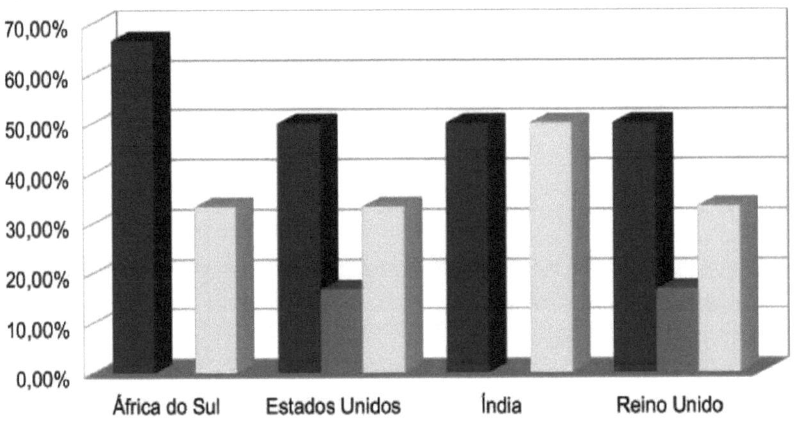

Figura 6 - Adherence to the guidelines of the Cybersecurity Culture category

Looking at Figure 8, it can be seen that the Brazilian 'technical cooperation' guidelines do not adhere to any of the Indian policy guidelines, as there are no Indian guidelines in this category. Another point to note is that when analysing the relationship between Brazil and the United Kingdom, only one guideline has partial adherence, which deals with technical cooperation with local and civil actors, while the other guidelines encourage international cooperation, both in convincing people of the importance of the issue and in building a relationship of trust with the development of international rules and principles. The guidelines addressed by foreign countries that are not identified in the Brazilian PCD are:

- The guideline contained in the South African: Affiliating international organisations in order to promote coordinated global responses to threats and vulnerabilities and keeping those involved abreast and developing a cybersecurity front;

• And the directive contained in US policy: The official cyber security policy should help coordinate intelligence and military policies and strategies for cyberspace, including to combat terrorism and the use of the Internet to ensure the integration of the entire mission.

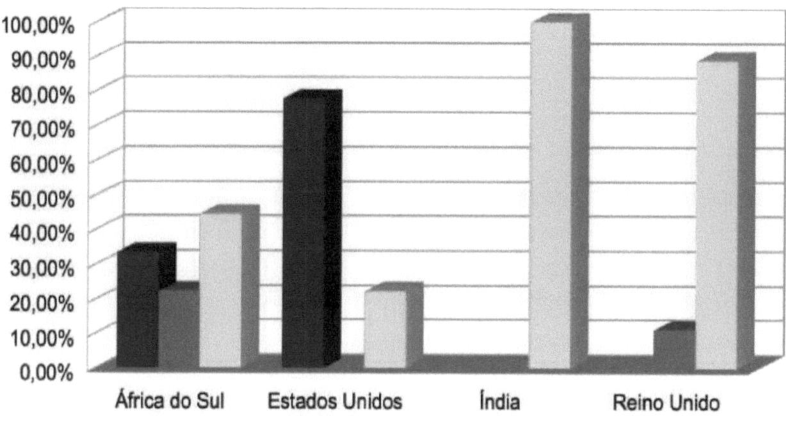

Figura 7 - Adherence to the guidelines of the Technical Cooperation category

In the category of 'security infrastructure', when comparing Brazil's policy with that of the countries analysed, we initially see that Brazil's policy is completely in line with that of the United Kingdom. The actions determined in both policies are guided by the creation of cyber intelligence structures aimed at developing and producing knowledge in the cyber sector, according to guideline BR-23: Create cyber intelligence structures, as required by the central intelligence bodies of the FAs and the SMDC, to apply scientific and systematic methods, seeking to extract and analyse data from the cyber source, producing knowledge of interest. The graph shows that there **is no adherence between** Brazilian policy and the other policies analysed, since they do not mention actions to create, develop or derive security infrastructures, so it can be seen that these countries apparently do not prioritise these actions.

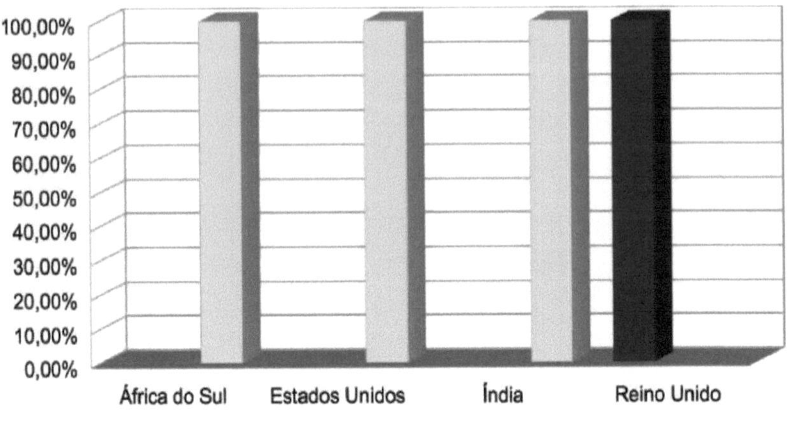

Figure 8 - Adherence to the guidelines of the Security Infrastructure category

The 'standardisation' category has a particular bias due to the issue of Brazil's cyber security coordination structure. When comparing Brazil with foreign countries, the difference in the coordination of strategic issues was highlighted, as for example Brazil separates its actions by assigning cyber security to the GSI body of the Presidency of the Republic and cyber defence to the Military Cyber Defence System (SMDC) and the Cyber Defence Centre (CDCiber) coordinated by the Brazilian Army and the Ministry of Defence in accordance with directive BR-43: Create the structure to carry out the coordination and integration of the cyber sector within the scope of the MD, as the central organ of the SMDC, with the possibility of participation by military personnel from the fa and civilians.

Unlike Brazil's policy, the policy of the United States of America establishes a central body for cyber security and defence with the Department of Defence (DoD) and within this structure cyber defence is divided into the *US Cyber Command* (USCYBERCOM) and cyber security into the *National Security Agency* (NSA), both within and with the same leader.

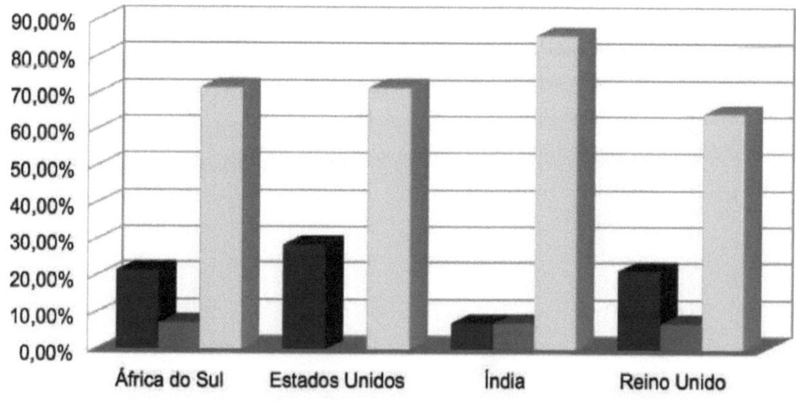

Figure 9 - Adherence to guidelines in the Standardisation category

The study of guidelines in the category of 'cyber security training' shows that South African and Indian policies do not adhere to guidelines for this category. The policies of the United States and the United Kingdom have guidelines contained in the category, but only some Brazilian policies adhere to them.

The Brazilian guidelines focus on training personnel to create a framework of knowledge and also on creating subjects in universities and colleges to help develop technical-scientific knowledge and encourage research in the cyber sector, in accordance with guidelines B-06: Include cyber defence content in the curricula of courses at all levels, where appropriate, of the MD's educational establishments and B-02: Continuously train personnel to work in the cyber sector, under the guidance of the SMDC's central body, taking advantage of existing structures.

Another point that is described in Brazil's policy guideline B-05: Create instruments to enable and motivate the permanence of specialised personnel in cyber sector activities, allowing for the continuity of the activity, mainly motivates those involved in the sector to train and motivate the development of the sectors of the APF that have critical infrastructures.

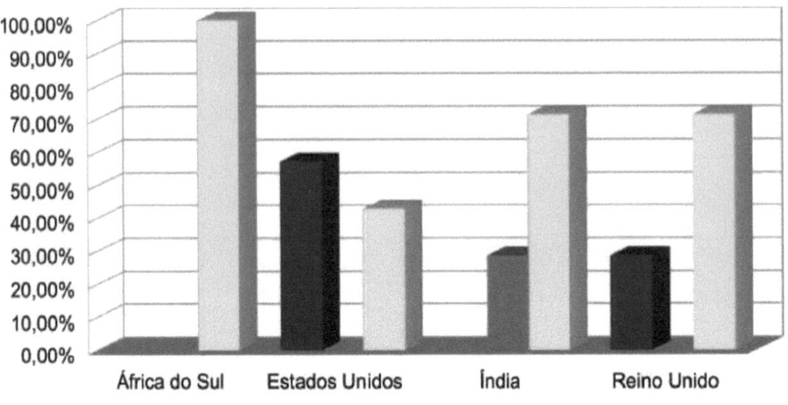

Figure 10- Adherence to the guidelines of the Cybersecurity Training category

5.2 SEMI-STRUCTURED INTERVIEW

As mentioned above, in order to integrate and improve the results of the content analysis, an interview was conducted with a specialist in the area, using the semi-structured interview technique, on the ninth of September, two thousand and thirteen. The interviewee has a short degree in Physical Sciences and Maths and specialises in Information and Communications Security Management. He has been working in the area of cyber security for over seven years and is a member of the Information Security Management Committee - CGSI (a body of the Executive Secretariat of the National Defence Council) and the ICP-Brasil Management Committee, working mainly on the following topics: internet, politics and government, information security, governance and economics.

The interview script was created based on the categories defined in the content analysis. Each category covers specific aspects of the guidelines of the Cyber Security Policies analysed, which were assessed in terms of their adherence to the guidelines of Brazil's Policy.

The interview with a specialist in the cyber sector was important for deducing adherence to the guidelines of Brazil's Cyber Defence Policy, as it allowed the professional to speak freely on the subject in question, as well as giving the interviewer flexibility to explore the issues. Divergent issues were included in this script with greater emphasis in order to ascertain the opinion of the specialist in the area on these comparisons and their approaches in the Brazilian cyber defence policy, also checking on issues dealt with in the policies of foreign countries that are absent from the Brazilian one and thus observing how this issue could be dealt with in their PCD. This script served as a guide for the semi-structured interview and can be seen in Appendix 7.

The professional interviewed has not been identified by name in the results, as this was previously communicated when contacting him, and his permission was obtained to transcribe the interview as a whole. The interview was recorded and transcribed in Appendix 8. It lasted approximately sixty (60) minutes and even though it was an informal technique, the proposed interview script was fully covered during the interview. As it was semi-structured, the interview allowed responses to be monitored and, when necessary, related questions were asked that were not included in the original script. As recommended by Bardin (2011), this helped to uncover additional information.

Initially, the interview sought to verify the subject with a general approach, i.e. without raising the issues pointed out in the content analysis. The interview also sought to raise questions about the understanding of the subject within the federal public administration. Finally, the interview asked him about the items and the adherence to the policies studied in this paper. With the results of the interview and the content analysis, we proceeded to evaluate this information, with the aim of achieving the objectives of this study, as presented in the next section.

5.3   ANALYSING THE RESULTS

The interview was enlightening and supported various points that were addressed in the analysis. These observations were collated one by one with the results of the analysis to reach definitive conclusions.

It is worth noting that the interview highlighted some of the main results obtained by applying the content analysis technique, such as:

- International co-operation' is important for the country's development in the cyber security sector because, as shown in the content analysis, the policies of the countries studied address affiliation with international organisations for the development of techniques, models and awareness in the cyber sector;

- 'Cybersecurity training' for actors involved in the APF to foster the creation of a knowledge framework characterised by Brazilian cyber policy in the following guidelines BR-01 and BR-02: Identify, register and select personnel with competences or skills, existing in the internal and external environments of the armed forces, to join the SMDC; and Continuously train personnel to work in the cyber sector, under the guidance of the SMDC central body, taking advantage of existing structures;

- Creation of a 'cyber security culture' to support the evolution in the use of critical infrastructure services focussed on the policies of Brazil and South Africa in guidelines BR-17: Encourage the development and exchange of theses, dissertations and other similar work, with a doctrinal focus, in civilian and military higher education institutions of interest to cyber sector activities; and ZA-09: Promote the development and research capacity of a cyber security agenda and improvement with South African Universities, industries and the Department of Science and Technology;

In Brazil, the structure adopted for cyber adaptation is different from the actions being taken by other countries. The first point observed was that the institutional structure of the countries analysed is noteworthy. While in foreign countries cyber security and defence have a single leadership, in Brazil they have been separated. Brazil has segregated the direction of information security and cyber defence actions into two distinct and independent bodies, GSI/PR and CDCiber/EB/MD respectively. This configuration tends to weaken both the defence and cybersecurity programmes because, as well as isolating them, they both depend on the affinity, integration and collaboration of the heads of these institutions. Each organisation reports on its work in different ways and to different authorities, and this makes long-term joint actions difficult.

In the category of 'information security', the analysis of the guidelines of the countries analysed showed that Brazil does not address respect for the individual right to privacy of the actors involved, while the other policies studied addressed the issue within their scope. This can be seen, for example, in guideline US-42: Implementing high-value activities, an *OPT-IN*, which corresponds to the set of rules according to which marketing or commercial messages are only sent to those who have previously and explicitly expressed their consent, of the interoperable identity matrix management systems to build trust for online transactions and to improve privacy. At the time this analysis was made in the interview, the interviewee provided information that although it is mentioned in the policies of foreign countries and not addressed in Brazilian policy, Brazil is innovating with the Marco Civil da Internet, which is an important point for the rest of the world, but from the point of view of those who operate the law, it is complicated. The Brazilian Congress is there to guide what's good for the country, but it's a big step forward for individual rights and, on the other hand, it will help to reduce electronic and cyber crime. The interviewee also noted that the regulation of individual rights should be regulated by the Brazilian National Congress.

Disaster recovery was again not a point addressed in Brazil's policy, but it was addressed in the US policy in US-41, which reads as follows: Develop solutions for emergency communications resources during a period of natural disaster, crisis or conflict, ensuring net neutrality. According to the interviewee, this type of concern on the part of Brazil exists despite not being listed as a guideline in the policy. One of the actions involving this is the creation of incident response teams to create methodologies with the GSI in federal public administration bodies. Mandarino Junior and Canongia (2010) point to the limited range of national critical infrastructures already prioritised and the insufficient number of computer network incident response and handling teams in the various segments of society, as well as the insufficient number of specialists with the skills to carry out such activities, as problems to be solved.

When analysing the 'interaction with other bodies and actors' category, it was found that there is a guideline in Brazilian policy that addresses combat operations and simulations in conjunction with these actors involved, and by checking with the interviewee, it was observed that although the countries analysed do not address this in their policies as a guideline, they do adopt these types of cyber combat exercises. This type of action is not seen as a guideline by the interviewee, but it is important for the development of the cyber sector. According to Mandarino and Canongia (2012), Brazil's creation of the National Critical Infrastructure Security Plan (PNSIEC) provides for the establishment of an integrated process, through the creation of a culture of security and protection, in all spheres of power, of qualified human resources, equipment, facilities, knowledge, services, routines, data, information and strategic processes, and seeks to extend the effort of the initiatives to the private sector.

The creation and maintenance of situational awareness about risk in cyberspace as a guideline for a security policy, analysed in the category of 'cybersecurity culture', is only dealt with in South African policy. This can be seen in Figure 7 and this guideline is seen as so important by the interviewee that it should start at school, the Ministry of Education and Culture (MEC) should play a very big role in bringing this issue of protecting individual rights, protecting information into schools. The interviewee has been talking to the MEC about including this issue in the curriculum, but there are many priorities. This awareness doesn't just have to reach the DSIC or APF, it has to reach the student, the entrepreneur and the micro-entrepreneur. According to Mandarino Junior and Canongia (2010), some of the challenges in this category that must be overcome are:

- Lack of education and formation of a cyber security culture at all levels, basic, fundamental, technical, specialised, masters and doctorate;
- Incipient training of technicians, specialists, masters and doctors for basic and applied research, as well as for the production of cyber security prototypes;
- The country's primary and secondary school curricula do not necessarily cover topics such as information security and related issues, even though children and young people make heavy use of the Internet, particularly social networks.

Still in the same category, there is a guideline addressed only in the Brazilian PCD, when compared to the other foreign countries analysed, which is the identification of both individual and organisational competences, seeking partnerships and exchanges of cyber experiences. This action is analysed by the interviewee as not being the responsibility of the Ministry of Defence, but of the GSI, with interaction between the Ministries of Justice, the Ministry of Communications, the Ministry of Development and Trade and the Ministry of Science and Technology. These ministries have to add the idea of cyber security to their functions in order to help the actors involved in their activities. There are 18 standards that have been developed by the DSIC on information security, ranging from the Information and Communications Security Policy to the cryptography that should be used, and according to the interviewee, these bodies do not follow these standards.

The training of personnel in the cyber sector is another point observed that shows a difference in the approach of the policies analysed in the 'cyber security training' category. According to the interview, Brazil is ahead in this approach. The interviewee warns that it's important as a whole, Brazil today doesn't have enough network administrators, it doesn't have enough people with security composure, this is much more of the federal public administration, 6,000 public bodies, 1.6 million civil servants, most of them with a computer in front of them, all using mobile phones, pendrives, and counting the many outsourced workers, many fourth parties, and sometimes the security manager is held hostage by the government. So we realise that the reality is different, now we need to have a precise culture.

The interviewee explained that the area of Information Security is very sensitive and should follow the intelligence methods of Italy, where no one goes into the intelligence area through a public competition, people are invited, unlike what happens in Brazil. With the exception of Angola and Brazil, which have public competitions, where experts in the field think it's too risky, as anyone could gain access to this sector, whose only selection process is a knowledge test. In other countries, the person is recruited for the intelligence area. In Brazil, people should also be recruited for the area of information security. The interviewee doesn't trust or believe that someone will prove that a hacker is a person who can work in this area. A door-knocker being asked to be a locksmith is absurd and should be seen in the same way as a *hacker* being asked to be a Security Manager.

Within the scope of the creation of technical partnerships between civilians, public and private organisations for this development in the cyber sector with Brazil's APF, it can be seen that the Brazilian, South African and North American policies are the ones that address the issue in their guidelines, as we can see in BR-10: Create partnerships and cooperation between military research and development centres and civilian research and development centres (public and private), to stimulate the integration of initiatives of interest to St Cyber; in ZA-02: Coordinate and cooperate between the public sector, the private sector and civil society; and in US-04: The federal government should continue the "bridge mission" principle begun under CNCI. Departments and agencies should expand the sharing of experience, knowledge and perspectives on threats, technology and vulnerabilities among network defenders and intelligence, military and stakeholder organisations participating in US operational development in cyberspace. The interviewee explained that it is necessary to involve these actors not only to help develop the country's cyber security, but also to create awareness on the subject.

Analysing the partnership with civilians, Mandarino Junior and Canongia (2010) also list the incipient government actions to encourage the private sector to demand and fund research, development and production of cyber security solutions at universities or other centres of excellence and the lack of a specific programme that includes government actions, projects and funding that directly demand cyber security solutions at universities or other centres of excellence, through research, development and production of these solutions.

Analysing the guidelines of the 'technical cooperation' category revealed interesting points, especially regarding interaction with international strategic allies. The policies of foreign countries address international co-operation as part of the development of cyber security. In South Africa's policy, the subject of international cooperation was addressed in guideline ZA-04, which reads as follows: Affiliate international organisations in order to promote coordinated global responses to threats and vulnerabilities and keep those involved abreast and develop a cybersecurity front. United States policy directive US-17 addresses the following: Develop U.S. government positions for an international cybersecurity policy framework and strengthen our international partnerships to create initiatives that address the full range of activities, policies, and opportunities associated with cybersecurity. This type of international cooperation action has not been addressed in Brazilian policy, which could be a problem, since the interview provided for this work reported that international cooperation is fundamental, the country has to have this integration, because nobody knows how to defend themselves against it alone, nobody can defend themselves against it alone, nobody has the methodology created, etc. There is no "recipe for cake" so everyone is learning from everyone else, I think that because of Brazil's tradition, we shouldn't adopt a bloc or multilateral policy, Brazil has a tradition of bilateral agreements in this area. We're at a time when Brazil is favouring Mercosur, so we should cooperate with the other American countries too.

Mandarino Junior and Canongia (2010) describe that there are some challenges to be overcome, such as: the absence of specific international instruments against cybercrime for cross-border police action and the still incipient articulation in terms of defining transnational cyber security actions, with a focus on cybercrime.

CHAPTER 6

CONCLUSION AND PROPOSALS FOR FUTURE WORK

The main objective of this study is to evaluate Brazil's Cyber Defence Policy (CDP), to verify its adherence to the policies of other countries, with a view to enriching the discussion of future actions for the defence of Brazilian cyberspace. We can see that the literature review and the theoretical framework confirm the prominence of the subject on the world stage.

Due to the various cases of cyber security reported in the media, this term is currently much discussed by nations and scholars due to the espionage of information from their organisations. These discussions focus on how to act and how to prevent it. Despite some problems with the taxonomy on the subject, the idea of protecting information assets is generally approached from the same direction, as can be seen from the absence of conflicting guidelines in the policies analysed. One approach in all the policies analysed was to prioritise the protection of information, knowing that the importance is the same for all and that the three main objectives that need to be achieved are confidentiality, integrity and availability, which are the pillars of information security, in different doses according to the situation.

Brazil is a global player whose attention today is focused on technological development, both in the agricultural area and in the oil and oil products exploration sector. Given that this information is strategic for sustainable development and is part of the country's secret information park, it is necessary to build a national agenda of actions to comply with the guidelines set out in its Cyber Defence Policy.

It can still be seen that the terms and definitions are confused in their constitution, not only between countries, but also in academic works and various publications. These differences in understanding cause problems in the formation of a cyber security framework and, above all, in the formation of a concept. It is therefore important to align the taxonomy in order to aid understanding and the search for guidance.

The PCD is a decisive milestone in the national cyber security panel, as Brazil has made great strides compared to other nations. Some objectives deserve attention and urgency due to their importance as a factor in developing and updating the doctrine that will guide the actions and use of the cyber sector. This objective will make it possible to carry out combat simulation exercises and create a framework of knowledge on the subject to better prepare the actors involved.

When compared to other countries, it is clear that the Brazilian Cyber Defence Policy is well structured despite some details that need to be changed, but when looking at the modularisation of the structure, it is not possible to understand how this hierarchy works. In Brazil's case, the important thing is to create a central body to coordinate both Cyber Defence and Cyber Security, thus guiding actions and creating norms. What happens today is exactly the opposite, where each person responsible for their area makes decisions and does not know what is in their scope of work or what is being done by the other. The co-ordinated bodies would be the Federal Police, the Secretariat for Logistics and Information Technology (SLTI), the Federal Data Processing Service (SERPRO) and other actors directly involved.

Another necessary measure is the migration of responsibility for cyber defence from the Brazilian Army to the Ministry of Defence. This provision would be important as a matter of hierarchy, facilitating the integration of the armed forces to take the necessary actions in the cyber defence sector.

The creation of a cyber security policy in the country would help in the development and integration of FPA actors to apply one of the DSIC's most important missions, which is: to plan and coordinate the execution of cyber security and information and communications security activities in the federal public administration.

The ability of critical infrastructures to withstand attempted attacks is another factor that must be observed and, above all, always aimed at increasing this capacity, investing in new technologies and establishing rules and standards that underpin the actions to be taken. Despite the many practical obstacles in applying these guidelines, both private companies and government bodies must find ways to establish cyber security through the use of mechanisms and/or processes. The uptake of new communication technologies should also be studied before they are absorbed to check that their uptake will not jeopardise actions in the cyber sector.

As a subsequent step, it is important to develop technology for operating these sensitive systems, where sensitive, secret and even top-secret information passes through. The technology to be developed would cover not only *software*, but also *hardware,* especially that used to communicate this data and information. This action is of fundamental importance to protect Brazil from espionage innovations by countries interested in accessing its information networks.

The lack of mapping of information assets destined for critical infrastructure services is key to creating a vulnerable field of operations with various explicit threats that can be exploited to steal information and/or make the service unavailable. Brazil's exclusive initiative to implement the public key infrastructure (ICP Defence) is a worthwhile effort to guarantee the security, confidentiality and integrity of the data and information in these infrastructures. The main function of ICP Defence is to define a set of standards, techniques, practices and procedures to be adopted by accredited entities in order to establish a standard in the creation and maintenance of digital certificates. By defining this standard for the use of digital signatures, its implementation creates the necessary security conditions for bringing the government closer to citizens and the private sector, as well as bringing the private sector closer to citizens, more quickly and, above all, securely.

The involvement of both public and private civil partners helps to raise public awareness about cyber security and how people should protect their own internet data, promoting education and training. This prerogative must be addressed to promote a culture of cyber security in order to help develop a safer country. Actions could even be taken where the culture begins in basic school education, where children would already be aware of the importance of protecting their information. Not only in education, but also with technical co-operation agreements with universities and private companies to develop methodologies, equipment and technologies to support the cyber sector.

Disaster prevention is an important factor to be incorporated into cyber security policy, especially in the field of communications, to avoid the absence of part or all of this very important process, which is the exchange of information, ideas or messages. Brazilian policy does not incorporate this type of action into its guidelines to protect against this type of disturbance. The lack of access to communication channels between the actors involved is considerable, even if it occurs during a cyberwar. Without the basic and necessary means, it would be almost impossible to create or modify strategies, tactics, attack plans or defences.

International co-operation is an important factor in the development of cyber security in the countries involved. Like any alliance, co-operation must be based on a relationship of trust. A number of foreign countries create these co-operation agreements and spell out the importance of these actions in their cyber security policy guidelines. In the case of Brazil's PCD, this is not included in its scope, although the interview with a specialist in the area clarified that there are bilateral agreements with foreign countries, especially those located in South America.

The objective that will guide the training and management of the human talents needed to conduct the activities of the cyber sector must be carefully observed in order to identify, register and select the personnel with the competences or skills that exist in the internal and external environments of the federal government to help make up the SMDC.

In conclusion, it is understood that the guidelines adopted in Brazil's cyber defence policy are pertinent and very well guided, even if the policy does not address some of the points discussed in this work. All that should be done is to look at the relevance of the results obtained in this analysis in order to improve the scope of the Brazilian policy. On other points analysed, Brazil's policy is ahead of the other policies of the foreign countries analysed in this study.

An opportunity to evolve the study carried out in this dissertation would be to analyse the adherence of foreign countries' policy guidelines to the existing guidelines in Brazil's policy in order to make it more complete, exploring aspects that were outside the initial proposed objective.

In the study, adherence was checked in the comparison tables of the guidelines contained in Appendix 6, but these adherences were not analysed. Another proposal would be to compare the Cyber Security and Cyber Defence structures in the countries analysed with the structure adopted by Brazil, since this study only found that there is a difference and that it is not appropriate to the reality practised by foreign countries.

The proposal of a Cyber Security Policy for Brazil is yet another point that needs to be explored in order to better adapt institutional actions in the Federal Public Administration and segregate the Defence and Cyber Security functions.

Finally, research into the classification of levels of thought and the order of learning in the cyber sector is also proposed in order to level out the vocabulary and also to facilitate understanding, since it was observed in this study that some of the countries analysed use their own taxonomy, which ends up creating some confusion in academic studies.

CHAPTER 7

REFERENCES

ALVES JÚNIOR, Sérgio Antônio Garcia. **National Cyber Security Policies**: The Telecommunications Regulator - Brazil, the United States, the International Telecommunications Union (ITU). Brasília: UNB, 2011. 99 p. Dissertation (Master's) - Postgraduate Programme in Regulation and Business Management (REGEN), Faculty of Economics, Administration and Accounting (FACE), University of Brasília (UnB), Brasília, 2011.

Association for the Promotion and Development of the Information Society. **Glossary of the Information Society**. Portugal: APDSI. 2005. 151 p.

BAKER, Stewart; WATERMAN, Shaun; IVANOV, George. Under Crossfire: **Critical Infrastructure in the Age of Cyberwar.** McAfee, 2013. Available at: <http://www.mcafee.com/us/resources/reports/rp-in-crossfire-critical-infrastructure-cyber-war.pdf>. Accessed on: 07 October 2012.

BARDIN, Laurence. **Content analysis**. Editions 70, 1977. 221 p.

. **Content analysis**. Editions 70, 2011. 279 p.

BARROS, Aidil Jesus Paes de & SOUZA, Neide Aparecida de. **Fundamentos de Metodologia.** São Paulo: McGraw-Hill, 1986.

BECHARA, Marcelo. **The turn of the mobile network**. In: CGI.br (Brazilian Internet Steering Committee). Survey on the use of information and communication technologies 2009. São Paulo, 2010, pp. 81-85.

BERTONHA, João Fábio. A national defence policy. Meridiano 47. Ed. 103. Feb. 2009 24p.

BEZERRA, Marcelo. **Digital Security Blog: Cyber War**. Available at: <http://segdigital.blogspot.com.br/2009/08/cyberwar.html>. Accessed on: 9 January 2012.

BRAZIL. **Decree nº 6.703**, of 18 December 2008.

. Cabinet of Institutional Security, **Ordinance No. 45** of 8 September 2009.

. **Law no. 7.783**, of 28 June 1989.

. **National Defence Policy**. Decree No. 5.484, 30 June 2005. Brasília, DF, 2005.

. **Normative Ordinance No. 3.389**, of 21 December 2012.

. **Presidency of the Republic. Civil House**. Executive Committee for Electronic Government. Working Groups - Electronic Government, 2001.

CERT.br - **CERT.br announces 60 per cent reduction in Internet security incident notifications in 2010.** São Paulo, 2011 . Available at: <http://www.nic.br/imprensa/releases/2011/rl-2011-02.pdf>. Accessed on: 10 January 2012.

- **Statistics of Incidents Reported to CERT.br.** Available at: <http://www.cert.br/stats/incidentes/#2012>. Accessed on: 09 February 2013.

CETIC.br - Centre for Studies on Information and Communication Technologies. <http://cetic.br/empresas/2011/c-geral-07.htm>. Accessed on: 07 March 2013.

CGI.br - Brazilian Internet Steering Committee. **ICT Households and Businesses 2011 - Survey on the use of information and communication technologies in Brazil**. 2012. p. 608.

CRESPO, Marcelo Xavier de Freitas. **Digital Crimes**. São Paulo: Saraiva, 2011. 97 p.

CRUZ, Ricardo Henrique Paulino da. **CYBERNETIC SECTOR IN THE BRAZILIAN ARMY**, 2012 . Available at : <http://www.eceme.ensino.eb.br/ciclodeestudosestrategicos/index.php/CEE/XICEE/paper/vie w/25/49>. Accessed on 15 January 2012.

Cyberwar: Security, Strategy, and Conflict in the Information Age. Fairfax, VA: AFCEA International Press, 1996.

DE ÁVILA, Rafael Oliveira; DA SILVA, Rafael Pinto. INFORMATIONAL BRAZIL: CYBER

SECURITY AS A CHALLENGE TO NATIONAL SECURITY. **Politics and Economics of Information.** 151p.

DERTOUZOS, M. **O que será?** São Paulo: Companhia das Letras, 1997. 38 p.

DINIZ, Eli. Governability, Democracy and State Reform: The Challenges of Building a New Order in Brazil in the 90s. In: DATA - **Revista de Ciências Sociais.** Rio de Janeiro, volume 38, no. 3, 1995. p. 385-415.

ENCONTRO NACIONAL DE PESQUISA EM CIÊNCIA DA COMPUTAÇÃO, vol. 21, 2011, Brasília. Proceedings. Brasília: University of Brasília. 475 p.

ENDLER, Antônio Marcos. Governo Eletrónico: a internet como ferramenta de gestão dos serviços públicos. **Revista Eletrónica de Administração**, 4th edition, v. 14, 2001.

ESPINDULA, Victor Mateus. Cybersecurity: **Brazil's challenges in cyberspace**. Brazilian Seminar on International Strategic Studies SEBREEI. Porto Alegre, RS. Jun, 2012 . Available at: <http://www.ufrgs.br/sebreei/2012/wp-content/uploads/2013/01/Victor-Mateus-Espindula.pdf>. Accessed on: 12 January 2013.

UNITED STATES OF AMERICA. **Cyberspace Policy Review**: Assuring a Trusted and Resilient Information and Communications Infrastructure. Washington, DC: The White House. September 2009.

. **Remarks by the president on securing our nation's cyber infrastructure.**
Washington D.C.: The White House, 2009. Available at:<http://www.whitehouse.gov/thepressoffice/remarks-president-securing-our-nations-cyber-infrastructure>. Accessed on: 11 October 2011.

FAGUNDES, Renan Dissenha. Raphael Mandarino: Brazil can defend itself against virtual warfare. **Época,** September 2010 . Available at : <http://revistaepoca.globo.com/Revista/Epoca/0,,EMI175609-15224,00.html>. Accessed on: 28 April 2012.

FONTENELLE, Alexandre Scudiere. **Cyberspace on the International Agenda.** 2011.

GIL, Antonio Carlos. Methods and Techniques of Social Research. São Paulo: Atlas, 2008. 201 p.

GLENNY, Misha. **Dark Market: Cybercrime and You.** São Paulo: Companhia das Letras, 2011. 79p.

GONÇALVES, Alcindo. **How did the term "governance" come about?** USP, 2004. Available at: <http://www.conpedi.org.br/manaus/arquivos/Anais/Alcindo%20Goncalves.pdf>. Accessed on 20/08/2010.

GRILO, Margarida Maria Monteiro Marçal. **Interculturality in the contents of teacher training for the 1st cycle of basic education.**[o] 2012. Available at: <http://repositorio.ul.pt/handle/10451/8517>. Accessed on 04/09/2012.

HOSANG, Alexandre. National Cyber Security Policy: A Necessity for Brazil. **War College**, Rio de Janeiro, 2011.

HOUAISS, Antônio. Dictionary of the Portuguese language. **Rio de Janeiro, Objetiva,** 2001.2048 p.

HUNKER, Jeffrey. US International policy for cybersecurity: five issues that won't go away. **J. Nat'l Sec. L. & Pol'y**, v. 4, p. 197, 2010.

INDIA. **National Cyber Security Policy:** For secure computing environment and adequate trust & confidence in electronic transactions. May 2011.

LEMOS, André. Cyberspace and mobile technologies. Processes of territorialisation and deterritorialisation in cyberculture. **Image, visibility and media culture.** Book of the XV COMPÔS. Porto Alegre: Sulina, 2007. 17 p.

LÉVY, Pierre. Usina de Arte e Cultura Festival, in October 1994, Porto Alegre City Hall. **THE EMERGENCE OF CYBERSPACE AND CULTURAL MUTATIONS.** Available at: <http://www1.portoweb.com.br/pierrelevy/aemergen.html>. Accessed on 14 July 2012.

LEWIS, James A. **Securing Cyberspace for the 44th Presidency.** Centre for Strategic and International Studies , 2008. Available at : <http://csis.org/files/media/csis/pubs/081208_securingcyberspace_44.pdf>. Accessed on: 13 March 2012.

LIND, W. Understanding Fourth Generation Wars. **Military Review**, 2005. p. 12-17.

MAGNO, Alexandre et al. **Maturity Models**. UNEB, 2011. 11 p. Colegiado de Sistemas de Informação Universidade do Estado daBahia, Salvador, 2011.

MANDARINO JUNIOR, Raphael; CANONGIA, Claudia. **GREEN BOOK CYBERNETIC SECURITY IN BRAZIL**. Brasília, 2010. Available at: <http://dsic.planalto.gov.br/documentos/publicacoes/1_Livro_Verde_SEG_CIBER.pdf>. Accessed on: 10 November 2011.

. Cyber security: the challenge of the new Information Society. **Strategic Partnerships**, v. 14, n. 29, p. 21-46, 2009.

MEDEIROS, Paulo Henrique Ramos; GUIMARÃES, Tomás de Aquino. The institutionalisation of e-government in Brazil. **Revista de Administração de Empresas**, v. 46, n° 4, 2006.
MILAGRE, José Antonio. **Cyber War and Defence**. Available at: <http://josemilagre.com.br/blog/sala-de-estudos/cyberwar/pesquisas-2/guerra-e-defesa- cibernetica> Accessed on 23 February 2012.

MOREIRA, Joaqim M., **A Ética Empresarial no Brasil**.São Paulo: Pioneira, 1999.

MORESI, Eduardo; et al. **Cyber defence: a study on infrastructure protection and secure software**. Brasília, 2011. 141 p.

NATIONAL INFRASTRUCTURE PROTECTION PLAN. **Partnering to enhance protection and resiliency**. Department of Homeland Security (DHS), 2009. 12 p.

UNITED NATIONS. Benchmarking **E-Government: a global perspective.** New York: United Nations, American Society for Public Administration, 2002. 29 p.

NYE, Joseph. **War and peace in cyberspace**. O Estado de S. Paulo, 15 Apr. 2012, International, p. A22. Available at: <http://www.estadao.com.br/noticias/impresso,guerra- e-paz--no-ciberespaco-,861242,0.htm>. Accessed on 22 Feb. 2012.

NIST. **Cybersecurity Framework.** United States of America. 2013. Available at:

<http://www.nist.gov/itl/cyberframework.cfm> Accessed on: 07 March 2013.

OECD. **Cybersecurity Policy Making at a Turning Point**: Analysing a New Generation of National Cybersecurity Strategies for the Internet Economy. OECD, 2012. Available at: <http://www.oecd.org/sti/ieconomy/cybersecurity%20policy%20making.pdf>. Accessed on 12 February 2013.

PINHEIRO, Patrícia Peck. **Digital laws and their vulnerabilities.** Seminar on Cyber Security, 1, 2009, Brasília. **Proceedings.** Brasília: Army General Staff. 93 p.

PIERRE CALAME, André Talmant. **Questão do Estado no coração do futuro (a) - O mecano da governança,** p. 25, 2001, editora vozes.

REPUBLIC OF SOUTH AFRICA. **National Cybersecurity Policy Framework for South Africa.** Available at: <http://www.info.gov.za/speech/DynamicAction? pageid=461&tid=59794>. Accessed on 15 May 2011.

RIBEIRO, Sérgio Luís. **Strategy for the Protection of Critical Information Infrastructure and National Cyber Defence**. Strategic Challenges for Cyber Security and Defence. Presidency of the Republic, Secretariat for Strategic Affairs, 1ª edition, Brasília, 2011.

RICHARDSON, Roberto Jarry. **Social Research**. São Paulo: Atlas, 1985. 28 p.

ROSENAU, James N. **Governance, Order and Transformation in World Politics.** In: Rosenau, James N.; Czempiel, Ernst-Otto. **Governance without government: order and transformation in world politics.** Brasília: Ed. Unb and São Paulo: Imprensa Oficial do Estado, 2000. pp. 11-46.

SALOMÃO, Luiz Alfredo. **SAE emphasises the importance of cybersecurity awareness in society.** Secretariat for Strategic Affairs (SAE). Available at: <http://www.sae.gov.br/site/?p=4568>. Accessed on 01/03/2013.

SANTOS, Maria Helena de Castro. Governabilidade, Governança e Democracia: Criação da Capacidade Governativa e Relações Executivo-Legislativo no Brasil Pós-Constituinte. In: DATA - **Journal of Social Sciences**. Rio de Janeiro, vol. 40, n° 3, 1997. p. 335-376.

SCHNEIDEWIND, Norman F. Cyber Security Prediction Models. **The R & M Engineering Journal**, American Society for Quality, 2005.

SÚFFERT, Sandro. **Cyber Defence Policy**. Information Technology Blog. Available at: <http://sseguranca.blogspot.com.br/2012/12/politica-cibernetica-de-defence.html>. Accessed on 24/02/2013.

TEIXEIRA, Duda. A war for the internet. **Veja**, São Paulo, May 2007. 79 p.

TOMAR, Portugal. **Characteristics of the semi-structured interview**. 2008. Available at: <http://mariosantos700904.blogspot.com.br/2008/05/caractersticas-da-entrevista-semi.html>. Accessed on 13 March 2013.

INTERNATIONAL TELECOMMUNICATIONS UNION. **ITU Study on the Financial Aspects of Network Security**: Malware and Spam. Available at: <http://www.itu.int/ITU-D/cyb/cybersecurity/docs/itu-study- financial-aspects-of-malware-and-spam.pdf>. Accessed on: 12/03/2012

US lab develops federated model for defence against cyber attack, Network Security, Vol. 2009, n° 9, September 2009.

WHITE, Gregory B. The community cyber security maturity model. In: **Proceedings of the 40th Hawaii International Conference on System Sciences**, 2007.

. The community cyber security maturity model. In: **Technologies for Homeland Security (HST)**, 2011 IEEE International Conference. IEEE, 2011. p. 173-178.

Norton Study. **Consumer Cybercrime Estimated at $110 Billion Annually.** Symantec. Available at : <http://www.symantec.com/about/news/release/article.jsp?prid=20120905_02>. Accessed on 04 October 2012.

CHAPTER 8

APPENDIX 1

Guidelines and categories of PCD in Brazil.

Code	GUIDELINES	Categories
BR-01	Identifying, registering and selecting staff with competences or skills, existing in the internal and external environments of the organisations, to join the SMDC;	Cybersecurity Training
BR-02	Continuously train staff to work in St Cyber, under the guidance of the SMDC's central body, making use of existing structures;	Cybersecurity Training
BR-03	Make it possible for staff involved with St Ciber to take part in courses, internships, congresses, seminars, symposia and other similar activities in Brazil and abroad;	Cybersecurity Training
BR-04	Hold regular events to present and discuss relevant topics in areas of interest to the cyber sector, to be organised and led by the SMDC's central body, in order to level up and update knowledge;	Cybersecurity Training
BR-05	Create instruments to enable and motivate the retention of specialised staff in St Ciber's activities, allowing for continuity of activity;	Cybersecurity Training
BR-06	Include cyber defence content in the curricula of courses at all levels, where appropriate, of the MD's educational establishments.	Cybersecurity Training
BR-07	Adapt the intelligence doctrine to include the cyber source in the context of integrating data sources with a view to producing knowledge;	Cybersecurity Training
BR-08	Survey the critical information infrastructures associated with St Cyber to help build the situational awareness needed for cyber defence activities;	Technical Co-operation
BR-09	Realising strategic partnerships and exchanges between the fa and institutions of interest; and	Technical Co-operation
BR-10	Establishing a systemic/technical channel between the central body of the SMDC and the central intelligence bodies of the FAs, within the scope of SINDE, with regard to St Cyber; and	Technical Co-operation
BR-11	Create partnerships and cooperation between military research and development centres and civilian research and development centres (public and private), to encourage the integration of initiatives of interest to St Cyber; and	Technical Co-operation
BR-12	Create programmes within the MD, in partnership with the MCTI, that take into account the dual characteristics (civilian and military use) of information and communications technologies (IT) used in the cyber area, to strengthen the involvement of the industrial sector in the development phases of projects of interest to St Cyber.	Technical Co-operation
BR-13	Collaborate with the body of the Presidency of the Republic (PR) in charge of drawing up the national cyber security policy;	Technical Co-operation
BR-14	Collaborate, within the limits of the legislation in force, with the other bodies of the APF, upon request and through the PR, to re-establish cyber security;	Technical Co-operation
BR-15	Maintaining a database and establishing a systemic/technical channel between the SMDC central body and the APF bodies for sharing network incident information; and	Technical Co-operation
BR-16	Acting in the recognition of artefacts and the development of cyber tools, in conjunction with PR, contributing to the protection of the APF's information assets.	Technical Co-operation
BR-17	Encourage the development and exchange of theses, dissertations and other similar works, with a doctrinal focus, in civilian and military higher education institutions of interest to St Cyber's activities;	Cyber Security Culture
BR-18	Promote doctrinal, normative and technical exchanges with civilian and military institutions, both national and from friendly nations;	Cyber Security Culture
BR-19	Prospecting the needs of St Kitts and Nevis in the area of S,T&I, within the scope of defence, in order to identify the scientific and technological capacities needed to develop the sector;	Cyber Security Culture
BR-20	Identify specific competences (individual and organisational) in S,T&I, of interest to St Cyber, within the scope of the MD and civilian research and development centres (public and private), establishing partnerships between centres of excellence, at national level, to aggregate institutions and avoid the dispersion of resources;	Cyber Security Culture
BR-21	Propose to the federal government that a national education campaign on cyber defence be carried out, with the aim of mobilising the country to raise the level of awareness of Brazilian society.	Cyber Security Culture
BR-22	To know, through the PR, the critical information infrastructures of the APF bodies located outside the MD;	Cyber Security Culture
BR-23	Create cyber intelligence structures, as required by the central intelligence bodies of the FAs and the SMDC, to apply scientific and systematic methods, seeking to extract and analyse data from the cyber source, producing knowledge of interest;	Security infrastructure
BR-24	Establishing risk criteria inherent in information assets and managing them, reducing the risks to critical information infrastructures of interest to national defence to acceptable levels;	Interaction with other bodies and players
BR-25	Include cyber defence in combat simulation exercises and joint operations;	Interaction with other bodies and players
BR-26	Plan and execute the adaptation of science, technology and innovation (S,T&I) structures, integrating efforts between the FA to meet the needs of St Cyber;	Interaction with other bodies and players
BR-27	Create a permanent defence committee, made up of representatives of the MD and invited guests from other ministries and development agencies, to intensify and explore new opportunities for cooperation in S,T&I in areas of interest to St Cyber;	Interaction with other bodies and players
BR-28	Define the profiles of the personnel needed to carry out St Cyber's activities;	Standardisation
BR-29	Create specific positions and functions and staff them with specialised personnel to meet St Ciber's needs;	Standardisation
BR-30	Establish criteria and control the mobilisation and demobilisation of personnel for cyber defence activities;	Standardisation
BR-31	To create and standardise cyber security processes in order to standardise accreditation procedures within the scope of critical information infrastructures of interest to national defence; and to establish programmes/projects in order to ensure the capacity to act securely on the network, thereby strengthening the operability of the MD's command and control (c2) activity.	Standardisation
BR-32	Create the cyber defence doctrine at the proposal of the SMDC central body;	Standardisation
BR-33	Designate the central body of the SMDC as responsible for proposing innovations and doctrinal updates for St Cyber within the defence framework.	Standardisation
BR-34	To implement a defence CIS management methodology, taking into account current legislation and regulations, best practices, defence intelligence doctrine and international standards of interest;	Standardisation
BR-35	Keeping the cyber defence policy up to date in line with the national cyber security policy, when it exists;	Standardisation
BR-36	Defining roles and responsibilities for carrying out activities related to cyber defence;	Standardisation
BR-37	Drawing up proposals for the creation and adaptation of federal legislation to support cyber defence activities;	Standardisation
BR-38	Propose the creation of a budget programme to make St Ciber's actions and activities viable;	Standardisation
BR-39	Proposing the adaptation of the national mobilisation law and the national mobilisation system to make them compatible with the needs of St Ciber.	Standardisation
BR-40	Draw up mobilisation plans for information assets, with the respective costs, in line with the national mobilisation law;	Standardisation
BR-41	Adapting the SMDC's mobilisation needs to SINAMOB; and	Standardisation
BR-42	Designing and implementing the military cyber defence system (SMDC), with the participation of military personnel from the FA and civilians;	Information Security
BR-43	Create a structure to coordinate and integrate St Cyber within the MD, as the central body of the SMDC, with the possibility of military and civilian participation;	Information Security
BR-44	To survey critical information infrastructures associated with internal and external threats, whether real or potential, in order to help build the situational awareness necessary for intelligence activities.	Information Security
BR-45	Create a knowledge management system of lessons learnt to compose and update the doctrine; and	Information Security
BR-46	Implement a defence public key infrastructure (icp defence);	Information Security
BR-47	Determine interoperable defence cryptography standards in addition to those of the FA; and implement the defence sic audit system.	Information Security
BR-48	Revising the planning of employment hypotheses to take account of actions in cyberspace; and	Information Security
BR-49	Carry out a systematic survey of information assets that can be mobilised for St Cyber;	Information Security
BR-50	Draw up and keep up to date a database of information assets of interest to the mobilisation in favour of the SMDC;	Information Security

APPENDIX 2

South Africa's PCD guidelines and categories.

Code	GUIDELINES	CATEGORY
ZA-01	[CNCSC] To coordinate cyber security incident response activities in relation to national intelligence, national defence and cybercrime.	Technical co-operation
ZA-02	[CSIRTs] Co-ordinate and co-operate between the public sector, the private sector and civil society.	Technical co-operation
ZA-03	[NCSPF] Will provide for the establishment of collaboration with local stakeholders, and this collaboration will focus on: Inclusion of industry and creating an enabling environment for a successful partnership, Encouraging private sector groups with common security interests and collaborating with government including in the co-operation of industry groups, Bringing the private sector together with the public to hold forums and create a common sense of handling incidents and vulnerabilities.	Technical co-operation
ZA-04	Affiliation with international organisations in order to promote coordinated global responses to threats and vulnerabilities and to keep those involved abreast and develop a cybersecurity front.	Technical co-operation
ZA-05	[CSIRTs] Create and maintain situational awareness of risk in South African cyberspace	Cyber Security Culture
ZA-06	[CSIRTs] Initiate national cybersecurity awareness campaigns	Cyber Security Culture
ZA-07	Participate in regional, African Union and international forums on issues pertaining to cyber security to ensure South Africa's foresight in defining and drawing up a global cyber security agenda to combat cyber crime and build secure and reliable information technology centres.	Cyber Security Culture
ZA-08	Establishing bilateral and multilateral partnerships of national interest with various instruments such as memoranda of understanding, conventions and treaties.	Cyber Security Culture
ZA-09	[NCSPF] Promote the development and research capacity of a cyber security agenda and improvement with South African Universities, industries and the Department of Science and Technology.	Cyber Security Culture
ZA-10	[NCSPF] Implement cyber security awareness programmes for private sector, public sector and civil society users.	Cyber Security Culture
ZA-11	[NCSPF] Encouraging companies to develop a cyber security culture,	Cyber Security Culture

ZA-12	'NCSPF] Support dissemination to civil society, children and individual users,	Cyber Security Culture
ZA-13	'NCSPF] Promote a comprehensive national awareness programme and guidelines	Cyber Security Culture
ZA-14	'NCSPF] Review and update existing privacy regime,	Cyber Security Culture
ZA-15	NCSPF] Develop awareness of cyber risks and available solutions	Cyber Security Culture
ZA-16	'CNCSC] Carry out regular assessment and testing of national critical infrastructures, including vulnerability, threat and risk assessments and penetration tests.	Security infrastructure
ZA-17	CNCSC] Coordinate cyber security audits, assessments and exercises and assist in the development of a national defence plan.	Security infrastructure
ZA-18	'NCSPF] Develop the regulation of an integration framework for cryptography in the republic.	Security infrastructure
ZA-19	NCSPF] To develop Electronic Identity and a Public Key Infrastructure to guarantee: Authentication, Confidentiality, Integrity, Non-repudiation and the structure and regulation of the framework.	Security infrastructure
ZA-20	'NCSPF] Promote the continuous monitoring, review and application of regulatory frameworks that support cyber security	Security infrastructure
ZA-21	'CNCSC] To act as the single point of contact on cyber security matters relevant to national security (national defence, national intelligence and cyber crime)	Interaction with other bodies and players
ZA-22	'CNCSC] To facilitate the sharing of information and the exchange of technologies relevant to national security in cyberspace.	Interaction with other bodies and players
ZA-23	'CNCSC] Facilitate interaction, both nationally and internationally, including through international associations of organisations such as the Incident Response Forum and security teams (first), and develop a policy to inform such interaction (second).	Interaction with other bodies and players
ZA-24	CSIRTs] Disseminate relevant CSIRTs information to the NCSC or other sectors if necessary,	Interaction with other bodies and players
ZA-25	'CSIRTs] Act as a single point of contact for this specific sector on cybersecurity issues	Interaction with other bodies and players
ZA-26	'CSIRTs] Establish information exchange of processes and procedures with CNCSC as part of South Africa's National Cyber Security Coordination.	Interaction with other bodies and players
ZA-27	CSIRTs] Facilitate the exchange of technology and information between the sectors involved	Interaction with other bodies and players
ZA-28	'NCII] Facilitate a public-private partnership to implement a protection plan for critical information infrastructures.	Interaction with other bodies and players
ZA-29	CNCSC] Setting and guiding standards and best practices for South Africa	Standardisation
ZA-30	'CNCSC] Develop measures in line with cyber security issues that impact on national security	Standardisation
ZA-31	CNCSC] Facilitate the identification, protection and development of national standards on the protection and security of National Critical Infrastructure (NCII) information.	Standardisation
ZA-32	'CNCSC] Assist in Corporate Security and policy development, Governance, Risk Management and Compliance, Identity and security management, Information Security and event management and Digital Forensics	Standardisation
ZA-33	'CNCSC] Develop response protocols to guide coordinated responses to cybersecurity incidents with the various stakeholders, such as the National CSIRTs of cybersecurity entities in general.	Standardisation
ZA-34	CSIRTs] Develop measures to deal with the impact of cyber security on this sector	Standardisation
ZA-35	NCII] Development of regulations for the National Critical Information Infrastructure (NCII): Information Security Policy and procedures, Third-party access to the NCII, Access and authentication in the NCII, Database archiving and storage, Incident and business continuity management, and Physical and technical protection of the entire NCII.	Standardisation
ZA-36	'NCSPF] Review current legislation and regulations on cryptography.	Standardisation
ZA-37	'NCSPF] Promote appropriate international recognition and respect for cyber security standards. The Ministry of Communications should create appropriate standards and consult with the National Cyber Security Council.	Standardisation
ZA-38	The Crime Prevention and Security Justice body, with the help of other government bodies, will implement the cyber security policy to ensure centralised coordination.	Information Security
ZA-39	A Cybersecurity Response Committee chaired by the State Security Agency will be established within the Crime Prevention and Security Justice body to coordinate cybersecurity activities.	Information Security
ZA-40	0 National Cyber Security Coordination Centre (CNCSC), which will be established by the PCJS, will play a supervisory and coordinating role in operations in all Security Incident Response Groups.	Information Security
ZA-41	0 CNCSC will provide national guidelines and standards on the establishment of CSIRTs with a special focus on national security issues.	Information Security
ZA-42	CNCSC] Perform any other function consistent with the objectives defined in the policy	Information Security
ZA-43	CSIRTs] Conduct cybersecurity readiness audits, assessments and exercises for the sector	Information Security
ZA-44	NCSPF] To promote the capacity to develop South African strategies in specific skills to meet the growing challenges of dealing with cyber security threats.	Information Security
ZA-45	'NCSPF] Promote the capacity to recruit and retain strategists in order to ensure the technical level for the development of the republic's cyber security needs.	Information Security
ZA-46	'NCSPF] Promote the development and/or adoption of South African standards and international standards bodies to secure cyberspace and thus leverage e-commerce and the information society.	Information Security

APPENDIX 3

Guidelines and categories of PCD in the United States of America.

Code	GUIDELINES	Category
US-01	Expand support for key education and research and development programmes to ensure that the nation continues to have the capacity to compete in the information age economy.	Cybersecurity Training
US-02	Develop a strategy to expand and train the workforce, including attracting and retaining cybersecurity expertise from the federal government.	Cybersecurity Training
US-03	Establish an inter-institutional Information and Communications Infrastructure Policy Committee (ICI-IPC), chaired by the National Security Council (NSC) and Homeland Security Council (HSC), as the primary policy coordination body for issues related to the realisation of an assured, reliable, secure and survivable global information and communications infrastructure and related capabilities.	Technical co-operation
US-04	0 he federal government should continue the "bridge mission" principle begun under CNCI. Departments and agencies should expand the sharing of experience, knowledge and perspectives on threats, tradecraft, technology and vulnerabilities between network defenders and intelligence, military and law enforcement organisations developing operational US capabilities in cyberspace.	Technical co-operation
US-05	The official cyber security policy should help coordinate intelligence and military policies and strategies for cyberspace, including to combat terrorism the use of the Internet to ensure the integration of the entire mission	Technical co-operation
US-06	The official cybersecurity policy should analyse the responsibilities of these bodies and propose the necessary changes to optimise advice and eliminate unnecessary duplication.	Technical Co-operation
US-07	The federal government cannot succeed in many facets of securing cyberspace if it operates in isolation.	Technical Co-operation
US-08	Initiate a national public awareness and education campaign to promote cybersecurity	Cyber Security Culture
US-09	Build a cybersecurity-based vision of identity management and strategy that addresses privacy in the interest of civil liberties, leveraging privacy-enhancing technologies for the nation.	Cyber Security Culture
US-10	Determine the most efficient and effective mechanism for obtaining strategic warning, maintaining situational awareness, and informing incident response capability.	Cyber Security Culture
US-11	Signalling to the world that you are serious about tackling this challenge with strong leadership and vision	Cyber Security Culture
US-12	Discuss what the nation can do to solve problems in a way that the American people can appreciate the need for action.	Cyber Security Culture
US-13	0 federal government should initiate a national public awareness and education campaign informed by previous successful campaigns	Cyber Security Culture
US-14	Develop a workforce of US citizens needed to compete on a global level and sustain that leadership position.	Cyber Security Culture
US-15	The official cyber security policy, through the development of guidelines, should prepare for the president's consideration of an updated national strategy to protect information and communications infrastructure.	Cyber Security Culture
US-16	Convene inter-agency mechanisms necessary to conduct interagency legal analyses of priority cybersecurity-related issues identified during the development policy formulation process and formulate coherent unified policy guidance that clarifies the roles, responsibilities, as well as the application of agency authorities for cybersecurity-related activities across the federal government.	Interaction with other bodies and players
US-17	Develop US government positions for an international cyber security policy framework and strengthen our international partnerships to create initiatives that address the full range of activities, policies and opportunities associated with cyber security.	Interaction with other bodies and players
US-18	Develop a process between the private sector, the government and help to prevent, detect and respond to cyber incidents.	Interaction with other bodies and players
US-19	Expand information sharing on network incidents and vulnerabilities with allies and seek bilateral and multilateral agreements that will improve economic and security interests while protecting civil liberties and privacy rights.	Interaction with other bodies and players
US-20	Encourage collaboration between academic and industrial laboratories to develop path migration and incentives for the rapid adoption of technology development research and innovation.	Interaction with other bodies and players
US-21	Leadership must be high and strongly anchored within the White House to guide, coordinate action and achieve results	Interaction with other bodies and players
US-22	Clarification of the related cyber security roles and responsibilities of federal government departments and agencies, providing the policy, legal frameworks and necessary coordination to enable them to fulfil their missions.	Interaction with other bodies and players
US-23	0 President should consider appointing a cybersecurity policy officer in the White House, who would report to the NSC and accumulate duties with the NEC, to coordinate the Nation's cybersecurity-related policies and activities. This individual would chair the ICI-IPC and lead a robust process in consultation with other EOP elements to resolve competing priorities and coordinate interagency cybersecurity policy and strategy development.	Interaction with other bodies and players
US-24	Designate cyber security as one of the President's main management priorities and establish performance metrics.	Standardisation
US-25	Designate an official privacy and civil liberties body for the cybersecurity directorate of the NSC.	Standardisation
US-26	Prepare a cyber security incident response plan and start a dialogue to improve public-private partnerships with an eye to rationalisation, aligning and offering resources to optimise their contribution and engagement.	Standardisation
US-27	Improve the resolution process between agencies on interpretations of the law and application of policy and the authorities for cyber operations.	Standardisation
US-28	Use the infrastructure objectives and research and development framework to set targets for national and international organisations.	Standardisation
US-29	The official cybersecurity policy should be involved in all economic measures, counter-terrorism, science and technology policy and decisions to inform them from a cybersecurity perspective.	Standardisation
US-30	The president's policy must have clear presidential support, sufficient authority and resources to operate effectively in the formulation of policies and the coordination of activities related to cyber security in the interagency.	Standardisation
US-31	The official cyber security policy must be supported by at least two Directors General and appropriate NSC staff, and of course at least one Senior Director together with NEC staff.	Standardisation
US-32	The official cyber security policy should not have the operational responsibility or authority to make policy unilaterally	Standardisation
US-33	Appoint a body in accordance with the cyber security policy responsible for coordinating the nation's policies and activities.	Information Security
US-34	Establishing a strong relationship, under the direction of the cybersecurity policy officer, it will accumulate functions with the NSC and the NEC, to coordinate the inter-institutional development of cybersecurity-related strategy and policy.	Information Security
US-35	Protecting information and communications infrastructure, this strategy must include the continuous evaluation of activities in the CNCI and, where necessary, building on its successes.	Information Security
US-36	Develop a framework for research and development of strategies that technologies have the potential to increase the focus on the game-changing security, reliability, resilience and dependability of digital infrastructure;	Information Security
US-37	Provide research into event data to facilitate the development of tools, test community theories and identify viable solutions.	Information Security
US-38	Use OMB's programme evaluation framework to ensure that departments and agencies use performance-based budgets in pursuit of cyber security objectives.	Information Security
US-39	Develop a set of threat scenarios and metrics that can be used for risk management decisions, recovery planning and S&T prioritisation.	Information Security
US-40	Develop mechanisms for sharing information related to cyber security that respond to concerns about privacy and confidential information and make information sharing mutually beneficial.	Information Security
US-41	Developing solutions for emergency communications resources during a period of natural disaster, crisis or conflict, guaranteeing net neutrality.	Information Security

US-42	Implementing high-value activities (e.g. the Smart Grid), an opt-in identity matrix and interoperable management systems to build trust for online transactions and to improve privacy.	Information Security
US-43	Improve government procurement strategies and market incentives for flexible hardware and software insurance, security innovations, and secure management services.	Information Security
US-44	Having the responsibility to protect and defend the country, and all levels of government have the responsibility to guarantee the security and well being of citizens.	Information Security
US-45	The regional and functional directorate must designate a person to be responsible for monitoring issues related to cybersecurity in the directorate's portfolio and coordinating with the cybersecurity directorate.	Information Security
US-46	The national strategy must focus senior leadership attention and time on resolving the issues that hamper US efforts to achieve reliable, resilient global information security factors and related communications infrastructure and technological capabilities	Information Security

APPENDIX 4

Indian PCD guidelines and categories.

Code	GUIDELINES	Categories
IN-01	Identify members of management who have knowledge of the nature of the security problems and related information and designate them as your Point of Contact.	Cybersecurity Training
IN-02	Maintaining a level of knowledge necessary for self-protection	Cybersecurity Training
IN-03	Enunciating the national information security policy and coordinating all aspects of information security governance in the country.	Cyber Security Culture
IN-04	Creating the necessary situational awareness of threats to ICT infrastructure in order to determine and implement an appropriate response.	Cyber Security Culture
IN-05	Creating a cybersecurity culture of responsible user behaviour and actions.	Cyber Security Culture
IN-06	Identifying national security organisations and coordinating matters related to information security in the country.	Interaction with other bodies and players
IN-07	Catalyse activities of strategic importance to the nation related to cyber defence	Interaction with other bodies and players
IN-08	Expansion of the Cyber Warning and Information Network to support the government's role in coordinating crisis management for cyberspace security;	Interaction with other bodies and players
IN-09	Implementing the organisation's security policies in line with international standards.	Standardisation
IN-10	Develop a comprehensive maintenance and repair policy to increase the availability of cyber resources for all users in an efficient manner.	Standardisation
IN-11	Creating a favourable legal environment in favour of safe cyberspace, adequate trust and confidence in electronic transactions, increased law enforcement resources that can enable responsible action by stakeholders and effective prosecution.	Standardisation
IN-12	Political actions, promotion that enable compliance with international safety best practices and conformity assessment (product, process, technology and people) and Incentives for compliance.	Standardisation
IN-13	Identify and classify critical information infrastructure facilities and assets.	Information Security
IN-14	Implement national security threat and vulnerability assessments to understand the real consequences	Information Security
IN-15	Law enforcement, information security incident handling and crisis management processes on a 24x7 basis.	Information Security
IN-16	Preparing and managing emergency communication crises, redundancy and disaster recovery plans, testing and evaluating plans, etc.	Information Security
IN-17	Periodically checking the levels of preparedness for critical information infrastructure emergencies and the recovery time in the event of cyber attacks.	Information Security
IN-18	Implementation of a system to contain, retrieve and recover data.	Information Security
IN-19	Carrying out information infrastructure audits on an annual basis, independent of IT security and the audit organisation.	Information Security
IN-20	Implement in accordance with the best international practices for security, quality of service and service level in accordance with the (SLAs) and demonstration.	Information Security
IN-21	Use safe products and services and skilled labour to keep crisis management and emergency response in line.	Information Security
IN-22	Use legal software and update at regular intervals.	Information Security
IN-23	Watch out for security traps, while adhering to security alerts on the Internet.	Information Security
IN-24	Ensuring the security of cyberspace, using the appropriate technology and, most importantly, involving the right types of people with the right awareness, ethics and behaviour.	Information Security
IN-25	Protection of IT and critical information and communication networks and gateways.	Information Security
IN-26	Putting in place a 24 x 7 cyber security mechanism for emergency response and resolution and crisis management through effective forecasting, prevention, protection, response and recovery actions.	Information Security
IN-27	Indian development of techniques and appropriate security boundary technology research, solution orientated research, proof of concept, pilot development and deployment of IT product/process security.	Information Security
IN-28	Carry out effective cyber crime prevention and prosecutorial actions.	Information Security
IN-29	Provide proactive preventive and reactive mitigation actions to reach and neutralise the sources of problems and support the creation of a global security eco-system, including public-private partnerships, information sharing, bilateral and multi-lateral agreements with overseas CERTs, security agencies and security companies etc.	Information Security
IN-30	Carrying out data protection while processing, handling, storing and transporting and protecting sensitive personal information to create the necessary environment of trust.	Information Security
IN-31	To identify the most dangerous classes of cyber security threats to the nation, in IT to analyse the most critical infrastructure vulnerabilities, and the most difficult cyber security problems.	Information Security
IN-32	Strengthen the capacity of critical ICT infrastructure to resist cyber attacks.	Information Security
IN-33	Minimise damage and recover in a reasonable timeframe.	Information Security
IN-34	Apply cybersecurity in IT training and exercises and business continuity depends on critical sector plans to assess the level of emergency preparedness of critical information infrastructures in resisting cyber attacks and minimising damage and recovery time in the event of cyber attacks occurring.	Information Security
IN-35	Carrying out analysis, surveillance and alert activities, enabling the exchange of information and facilitating restoration efforts.	Information Security
IN-36	Provide regular updates to senior management on the progress of the incident handling process.	Information Security
IN-37	Coordinate efforts to protect the country's critical information infrastructure and enable the development of skills in communication, interception, monitoring and early warning and vulnerability checks with the appropriate authorisation.	Information Security

APPENDIX 5

UK PCD guidelines and categories.

Code	GUIDELINES	Category
GB-01	Have the transversal knowledge, skills and capacity you need to support all our cyber security objectives.	Cybersecurity Training
GB-02	Recognise the limits of their competence in cyberspace	Cybersecurity Training
GB-03	Having the capacity - in terms of skills, technology, confidence and opportunity - to access cyberspace.	Cybersecurity Training
GB-04	Promote the development of a cadre of qualified cyber security professionals so that the UK continues to maintain an edge in this area.	Cybersecurity Training
GB-05	Engage outside law enforcement personnel to help fight cybercrime as part of the NCA unit	Cybersecurity Training
GB-06	Managing crucial skills and helping to develop a community of "ethical hackers" in the UK to ensure that our networks are robustly protected.	Cybersecurity Training
GB-07	Working internationally to develop international principles or "rules of the road" for behaviour in cyberspace	Technical Co-operation
GB-08	Work with other countries on confidence-building practices, measures to reduce the risk of escalation and avoid misunderstandings.	Technical Co-operation
GB-09	Work to convince other countries to develop compatible laws, so that cybercrimes can be prosecuted across borders and cybercriminals are denied refuge.	Technical Co-operation
GB-10	Work with internet companies to explore the potential of online sanctions for online offences.	Technical co-operation
GB-11	Promote greater levels of international co-operation and shared understanding on cybercrime as part of the process initiated by the London Conference	Technical Co-operation
GB-12	Fostering a vibrant and innovative cybersecurity private sector to share information about threats in cyberspace	Cyber Security Culture
GB-13	Encourage, support and develop education at all levels, essential key competences and R&D.	Cyber Security Culture
GB-14	To help mould an open, cyberspace-stable and vibrant society that the UK public can use safely and that supports open societies.	Cyber Security Culture
GB-15	Show tolerance and respect for diversity of language, culture and ideas	Cyber Security Culture
GB-16	We will use cyber-relevant sanctions to combat cyber-crimes, such as online bullying or Internet fraud.	Cyber Security Culture
GB-17	Working to raise awareness and to educate and empower people and companies to protect themselves online	Cyber Security Culture
GB-18	Provide clear cyber security advice for use by anyone using the internet so that people can decide how they want to use cyberspace, informed about the risks	Cyber Security Culture
GB-19	Improve the information available to people buying safety products by encouraging the development of safety kitemarks. BIS works with domestic, European and global trade standards organisations.	Cyber Security Culture
GB-20	Sensitise businesses to the threat and the actions they can take to protect themselves, including working across sectors of strategic importance to raise cyber security issues along their supply chains.	Cyber Security Culture
GB-21	Helping consumers respond to the cyber threats that will be the "new normal" by using social media to provide warnings about fraud or other online threats.	Security infrastructure
GB-22	Help people identify if their computers have been compromised and what they can do to resolve the compromise and protect themselves from future attacks	Security infrastructure
GB-23	Ensure that new national procedures for responding to cyber incidents (ensuring that essential services can be maintained or restored quickly) are fully tested, both within the UK and in exercises with international partners.	Security infrastructure
GB-24	Build and maintain secure government ICT networks.	Security infrastructure
GB-25	Sharpen our ability to identify the nature and attribution of cyber attacks.	Security infrastructure
GB-26	Establishing new operational partnerships with private sectors, building important information points in cyberspace	Interaction with other bodies and players
GB-27	Helping consumers respond to the cyber threats that will be the "new normal" by using the media to warn people about scams or other online threats.	Interaction with other bodies and players
GB-28	Working collectively to tackle the threat of criminals operating online.	Interaction with other bodies and players
GB-29	Supporting the work of all four NCA operational commands (borders, organised crime, economic crime and Child Exploitation and Online Protection - CEOP) by providing specialist support, intelligence and guidance.	Interaction with other bodies and players
GB-30	Support police forces across England and Wales to drive greater national capability on cybercrime, including through training law enforcement on cyber issues, and making sure links to related issues such as bullying or child exploitation are made.	Interaction with other bodies and players
GB-31	Ensure the best possible flow of information between police and ANC forces	Interaction with other bodies and players
GB-32	Supporting forces to move towards full reporting of online crime, helping them to identify good practices.	Interaction with other bodies and players
GB-33	Working with consumers, we need to raise awareness in the business of the potential threat to reputation, revenue and intellectual property from a cyber attack.	Interaction with other bodies and players
GB-34	Enable the UK's cyber security industry to thrive and expand, supporting it in accessing markets abroad.	Interaction with other bodies and players
GB-35	Encouraging industry-led standards and guidelines that are easily used and understood, and that help companies that are good at security make that a selling point.	Interaction with other bodies and players
GB-36	Working with allies to ensure the implementation of NATO's cyber defence policy	Interaction with other bodies and players
GB-37	Creating and building a dedicated and integrated civilian and military capability within the Ministry of Defence. Cyber integration within the organisation and creation of a Defence.	Interaction with other bodies and players

GB-38	Strengthen international systems to build trust between states in cyberspace, including through engagement within the OSCE on confidence-building measures.		Interaction with other bodies and players
GB-39	Encourage industry-led standards and guidelines		Standardisation
GB-40	Create specific law to give cybercrime investigation capacity to the new National Crime Agency		Standardisation
GB-41	Encourage the use of "cyber-specialists" to make more use of those with specialised skills to help the police.		Standardisation
GB-42	Make sure that we can co-operate in law enforcement and deny refuge to cyber criminals.		Standardisation
GB-43	Modelling cybersecurity best practices on the government's own systems, setting strong standards for government suppliers to ensure they raise the bar.		Standardisation
GB-44	Ensuring the UK has a solid legal framework that allows law enforcement agencies to combat cybercrime.		Standardisation
GB-45	Work to ensure that law enforcement agencies and the judiciary are aware of the additional powers the courts already have to protect the public when there is great reason to believe that someone may commit more serious cybercrimes.		Standardisation
GB-46	Include restrictions on the use of the internet are used to protect the public or victims in cases of sexual crimes, harassment and anti-social behaviour, through guidance that will encourage the judicial system to consider these cyber-relevant sanctions for cyber offences where appropriate.		Standardisation
GB-47	Boost work on online crime design, development of best security practices, and effective crime prevention advice for all levels of business.		Standardisation
GB-48	Take steps to make sure that it is simple and straightforward for members of the public to report cybercrime, of course this should include the possibility of doing so online.		Standardisation
GB-49	Looking at the best ways to improve cyber security education at all levels so that people are better equipped to use cyberspace safely.		Standardisation
GB-50	Stimulating the development of industry-led standards and guidance that help customers navigate the market and differentiate companies with adequate levels of protection and good cyber security products.		Standardisation
GB-51	Helping consumers and small businesses navigate the market by encouraging the development of clear indicators of good cyber security products.		Information Security
GB-52	Carry out a professional strategy in business services, including insurers, auditors, and lawyers to determine the role they can play in promoting better cyber risk management.		Information Security
GB-53	Build an effective, easy-to-use, simple point to report cyber fraud and improve the police response at a local level for those who are victims of cyber crime		Information Security
GB-54	Fight cybercrime and be one of the safest places in the world to do business in cyberspace		Information Security
GB-55	To be more resistant to cyber attacks and better able to protect our interests in cyberspace.		Information Security
GB-56	Act proportionately in cyberspace, and in accordance with national legislation and international law		Information Security
GB-57	Ensuring that cyberspace remains open to innovation and the free circulation of ideas, information and expression.		Information Security
GB-58	Respect individual privacy rights and provide adequate protection for intellectual property.		Information Security
GB-59	Creation of a competitive environment that guarantees a fair return on investment in networks, services and content.		Information Security
GB-60	Improve our ability to defend against and deter high-end, state-sponsored threats, and to prevent these techniques becoming available to non-state actors.		Information Security
GB-61	Maintain an effective framework and enforcement capabilities to disrupt and prosecute cybercrime.		Information Security
GB-62	Ensuring that information intelligence is fed back into effective action and advice for the public.		Information Security
GB-63	Carry out underlying research and development to maintain the production of innovative solutions.		Information Security
GB-64	Creating a thriving market in cyber security products and services that can win the UK business abroad and contribute to growth.		Information Security
GB-65	Look closely at how intelligence (for example, on threats to children provided by CEOP) is used by forces and how the result of the action of the forces and the courts is fed back to develop the best possible picture on threats.		Information Security
GB-66	Provide facilities for the public to report crime online, although these range from basic systems for certain types of crime to fully integrated crime reporting tools.		Information Security
GB-67	Report fraud, including cyber fraud, via the internet using the Fraud Action tool.		Information Security
GB-68	Building our intelligence framework through the National Fraud Intelligence Bureau, improving the targeting of enforcement resources and feeding into crime prevention councils.		Information Security
GB-69	Finding ways to improve the profile and transparency of information on cyber security breaches.		Information Security
GB-70	Explore ways in which industry-led standards for companies' cyber security performance can be used as a general market benchmark		Information Security
GB-71	Review existing legislation, for example the Computer Misuse Act 1990, to ensure that it remains relevant and effective.		Information Security
GB-72	To explore ways in which GCHQ's expertise could more directly benefit economic growth and support the development of the UK's cyber security sector without compromising the security of the agency's core and intelligence mission.		Information Security
GB-73	Promote robust levels of cybersecurity in online public services, enabling people to transact online with the government with confidence.		Information Security
GB-74	Develop a better understanding of the cyber security industry's strengths, potential growth and barriers to success.		Information Security
GB-75	Develop a marketing strategy to promote the UK's cyber security capabilities internationally		Information Security
GB-76	Expand the government council to include a wide range of organisations whose resilience is a priority for the UK economy.		Information Security
GB-77	Maintaining and strengthening our ability to anticipate, prepare for and disrupt hostile acts in cyberspace (including improving information exchange across government and industry partners, improving defence against hostile acts and increasing law enforcement capacity to investigate and punish those who carry out hostile acts).		Information Security
GB-78	Maintain the capabilities that allow the Kingdom freedom of action and cyber advantage and preserve our sovereign capabilities in niche areas.		Information Security
GB-79	Supporting the application of research, working with the Government Office for Science and others to build innovative cyber security solutions, drawing on our world-leading technical resources in support of our national security interests and wider economic prosperity.		Information Security

APPENDIX 6

This appendix contains tables evaluating the guidelines contained in a specific category of Brazilian policy and those of one foreign country at a time.

Table 4 - Comparison of Cybersecurity Training in Brazil and the United States

ADHERENCE	CODE	GUIDELINES	CATEGORIA
		BRAZIL	
Non-adherence	BR-01	Identifying, registering and selecting staff with competences or skills, existing in the internal and external environments of the organisations, to join the SMDC;	Cybersecurity Training
Adhesion US-02	BR-02	Continuously train personnel to work in StCiber, under the guidance of the SMDC central body, making use of existing structures;	Cybersecurity Training
Non-adherence	BR-03	Make it possible for staff involved with St Ciber to take part in courses, internships, congresses, seminars, symposia and other similar activities in Brazil and abroad;	Cybersecurity Training
Non-adherence	BR-04	Hold regular events to present and discuss relevant topics in areas of interest to the cyber sector, to be organised and led by the SMDC's central body, in order to level up and update knowledge;	Cybersecurity Training
Adhesion US-02	BR-05	Create instruments to enable and motivate the retention of specialised staff in StCiber's activities, allowing for the continuity of the activity;	Cybersecurity Training
Adhesion US-01	BR-06	Include cyber defence content in the curricula of courses at all levels, where appropriate, of the MD's educational establishments.	Cybersecurity Training
Adhesion US-01	BR-07	Adapt the intelligence doctrine to include the cyber source in the context of integrating data sources with a view to producing knowledge;	Cybersecurity Training
		UNITED STATES	
Adherence	US-01	Expand support for key education and research and development programmes to ensure that the nation continues to have the capacity to compete in the information age economy.	Cybersecurity Training
Adherence	US-02	Develop a strategy to expand and train the workforce, including attracting and retaining cybersecurity expertise from the federal government.	Cybersecurity Training

Table 5 - Comparison of Cybersecurity Training in Brazil and India

ADHERENCE		GUIDELINES	CATEGORY
		BRAZIL	
Partial Adherence IN-01	BR-01	Identifying, registering and selecting staff with competences or skills, existing in the internal and external environments of the organisations, to join the SMDC;	Cybersecurity Training
Non-adherence	BR-02	Continuously train staff to work in St Cyber, under the guidance of the SMDC's central body, making use of existing structures;	Cybersecurity Training
Non-adherence	BR-03	Make it possible for staff involved with St Ciber to take part in courses, internships, congresses, seminars, symposia and other similar activities in Brazil and abroad;	Cybersecurity Training
Non-adherence	BR-04	Hold regular events to present and discuss relevant topics in areas of interest to the cyber sector, to be organised and led by the SMDC's central body, in order to level up and update knowledge;	Cybersecurity Training
Non-adherence	BR-05	Create instruments to enable and motivate the retention of specialised staff in St Ciber's activities, allowing for continuity of activity;	Cybersecurity Training
Non-adherence	BR-06	Include cyber defence content in the curricula of courses at all levels, where appropriate, of the MD's educational establishments.	Cybersecurity Training
Partial Adherence IN-02	BR-07	Adapt the intelligence doctrine to include the cyber source in the context of integrating data sources with a view to producing knowledge;	Cybersecurity Training
		INDIA	
Partial Adherence	IN-01	Identify members of management who have knowledge of the nature of the security problems and related information and designate them as your Point of Contact.	Cybersecurity Training
Partial Adherence	IN-02	Maintaining a level of knowledge necessary for self-protection	Cybersecurity Training

Table 6 - Comparison of Cybersecurity Training in Brazil and the United Kingdom

ADHERENCE	CODE	GUIDELINES	CATEGORY
		BRAZIL	
Adhesion GB-04 and 6	BR-01	Identifying, registering and selecting staff with competences or skills, existing in the internal and external environments of the organisations, to join the SMDC;	Cybersecurity Training
Non-adherence	BR-02	Continuously train staff to work in St Cyber, under the guidance of the SMDC's central body, making use of existing structures;	Cybersecurity Training
Non-adherence	BR-03	Make it possible for staff involved with St Ciber to take part in courses, internships, congresses, seminars, symposia and other similar activities in Brazil and abroad;	Cybersecurity Training
Non-adherence	BR-04	Hold regular events to present and discuss relevant topics in areas of interest to the cyber sector, to be organised and led by the SMDC's central body, in order to level up and update knowledge;	Cybersecurity Training
Non-adherence	BR-05	Create instruments to enable and motivate the retention of specialised staff in St Ciber's activities, allowing for continuity of activity;	Cybersecurity Training
Non-adherence	BR-06	Include cyber defence content in the curricula of courses at all levels, where appropriate, of the MD's educational establishments.	Cybersecurity Training
Adhesion GB-06	BR-07	Adapt the intelligence doctrine to include the cyber source in the context of integrating data sources with a view to producing knowledge;	Cybersecurity Training
		UNITED KINGDOM	
Adherence	GB-01	Have the transversal knowledge, skills and capacity you need to support all our cyber security objectives.	Cybersecurity Training
Non-adherence	GB-02	Recognise the limits of their competence in cyberspace	Cybersecurity Training
Non-adherence	GB-03	Having the capacity - in terms of skills, technology, confidence and opportunity - to access cyberspace.	Cybersecurity Training
Adherence	GB-04	Promote the development of a cadre of qualified cyber security professionals so that the UK continues to maintain an edge in this area.	Cybersecurity Training
Non-adherence	GB-05	Engage outside law enforcement personnel to help fight cybercrime as part of the NCA unit	Cybersecurity Training
Adherence	GB-06	Managing crucial skills and helping to develop a community of "ethical hackers" in the UK to ensure that our networks are robustly protected.	Cybersecurity Training

Table 7 - Comparison of Technical Cooperation between Brazil and South Africa

ADHERENCE	CODE	GUIDELINES	CATEGORY
		BRAZIL	
No Adherence	BR-08	Survey the critical information infrastructures associated with St Cyber to help build the situational awareness needed for cyber defence activities;	Technical Co-operation
Partially Adherent ZA-03	BR-09	Realising strategic partnerships and exchanges between the fa and institutions of interest; and	Technical Co-operation
Adherent ZA-02	BR-10	Establishing a systemic/technical channel between the central body of the SMDC and the central intelligence bodies of the FAs, within the scope of SINDE, with regard to St Cyber; and	Technical Co-operation
No Adherence	BR-11	Create partnerships and cooperation between military research and development centres and civilian research and development centres (public and private), to encourage the integration of initiatives of interest to St Cyber; and	Technical Co-operation
Adherent ZA-03	BR-12	Create programmes within the MD, in partnership with the MCTI, that take into account the dual characteristics (civilian and military use) of information and communications technologies (IT) used in the cyber area, to strengthen the involvement of the industrial sector in the development phases of projects of interest to St Cyber.	Technical Co-operation
No Adherence	BR-13	Collaborate with the body of the Presidency of the Republic (PR) in charge of drawing up the national cyber security policy;	Technical Co-operation
Adherent ZA-02	BR-14	Collaborate, within the limits of the legislation in force, with the other bodies of the APF, upon request and through the PR, to re-establish cyber security;	Technical Co-operation
Partially Adherent ZA-01	BR-15	Maintaining a database and establishing a systemic/technical channel between the SMDC central body and the APF bodies for sharing network incident information; and	Technical Co-operation
No Adherence	BR-16	Acting in the recognition of artefacts and the development of cyber tools, in conjunction with PR, contributing to the protection of the APF's information assets.	Technical Co-operation
		SOUTH AFRICA	
Partial Adherence	ZA-01	[Coordinate cyber security incident response activities in relation to national intelligence, national defence and cybercrime.	Technical co-operation
Adherence	ZA-02	[Coordinate and co-operate between the public sector, the private sector and civil society.	Technical co-operation
Adherence	ZA-03	[NCSPF] Will provide for the establishment of collaboration with local stakeholders, and this collaboration will focus on: Inclusion of industry and creating an enabling environment for a successful partnership, Encouraging private sector groups with common security interests and collaborating with government including in the co-operation of industry groups, Bringing the private sector together with the public to hold forums and create a common sense of incident and vulnerability handling.	Technical co-operation
No Adherence	ZA-04	Affiliation with international organisations in order to promote coordinated global responses to threats and vulnerabilities and to keep those involved abreast and develop a cybersecurity front.	Technical co-operation

Table 8 - Comparison of Technical Cooperation between Brazil and the United States

ADHERENCE	CODE	GUIDELINES	CATEGORY
		BRAZIL	
Adhesion US-07	BR-08	Survey the critical information infrastructures associated with St Cyber to help build the situational awareness needed for cyber defence activities;	Technical Co-operation
Adhesion US-04	BR-09	Realising strategic partnerships and exchanges between the fa and institutions of interest; and	Technical Co-operation
Adhesion US-04	BR-10	Establishing a systemic/technical channel between the central body of the SMDC and the central intelligence bodies of the FAs, within the scope of SINDE, with regard to St Cyber; and	Technical Co-operation
Adhesion US-03	BR-11	Create partnerships and cooperation between military research and development centres and civilian research and development centres (public and private), to encourage the integration of initiatives of interest to St Cyber; and	Technical Co-operation
Adhesion US-03	BR-12	Create programmes within the MD, in partnership with the MCTI, that take into account the dual characteristics (civilian and military use) of information and communications technologies (IT) used in the cyber area, to strengthen the involvement of the industrial sector in the development phases of projects of interest to St Cyber.	Technical Co-operation
Adhesion US-06	BR-13	Collaborate with the body of the Presidency of the Republic (PR) in charge of drawing up the national cyber security policy;	Technical Co-operation
Adhesion US-04	BR-14	Collaborate, within the limits of the legislation in force, with the other APF bodies, upon request and through the PR, to re-establish cyber security;	Technical Co-operation
No Adherence	BR-15	Maintaining a database and establishing a systemic/technical channel between the SMDC central body and the APF bodies for sharing network incident information; and	Technical Co-operation
No Adherence	BR-16	Acting in the recognition of artefacts and the development of cyber tools, in conjunction with PR, contributing to the protection of the APF's information assets.	Technical Co-operation
		UNITED STATES	
Adherence	US-03	Establish an inter-institutional Information and Communications Infrastructure Policy Committee (1C1-1PC), chaired by the National Security Council (NSC) and Homeland Security Council (HSC), as the primary policy coordination body for issues related to the realisation of an assured, reliable, secure and survivable global information and communications infrastructure and related capabilities.	Technical Co-operation
Adherence	US-04	0 he federal government should continue the "bridge mission" principle initiated under CNC1. Departments and agencies should expand the sharing of experience, knowledge and perspectives on threats, tradecraft, technology and vulnerabilities between network defenders and intelligence, military and law enforcement organisations developing operational US capabilities in cyberspace.	Technical Co-operation
No Adherence	US-05	The official cyber security policy should help coordinate intelligence and military policies and strategies for cyberspace, including to combat terrorism the use of the Internet to ensure the integration of the entire mission	Technical Co-operation
Adherence	US-06	The official cybersecurity policy should analyse the responsibilities of these bodies and propose the necessary changes to optimise advice and eliminate unnecessary duplication.	Technical Co-operation
Adherence	US-07	The federal government cannot succeed in many facets of securing cyberspace if it operates in isolation.	Technical Co-operation

Table 9 - Comparison of Cybersecurity Culture in Brazil and South Africa

ADHERENCE	CODE	GUIDELINES	CATEGORY
		BRAZIL	
Adhesion ZA-09	BR-17	Encourage the development and exchange of theses, dissertations and other similar works, with a doctrinal focus, in civilian and military higher education institutions of interest to St Cyber's activities;	Cyber Security Culture
Adhesion ZA-08	BR-18	Promote doctrinal, normative and technical exchanges with civilian and military institutions, both national and from friendly nations;	Cyber Security Culture
Adhesion ZA-09	BR-19	Prospecting the needs of St Kitts and Nevis in the area of S,T&I, within the scope of defence, in order to identify the scientific	Cyber Security Culture

ADHERENCE	CODE	GUIDELINES	CATEGORY
		and technological capacities needed to develop the sector;	
No Adherence	BR-20	Identify specific competences (individual and organisational) in S,T&I, of interest to St Cyber, within the scope of the MD and civilian research and development centres (public and private), establishing partnerships between centres of excellence, at national level, to aggregate institutions and avoid the dispersion of resources;	Cyber Security Culture
Adhesion ZA-10, 11, 12, 13 and 15	BR-21	To propose to the federal government that a national education campaign on cyber defence be carried out, with the aim of mobilising the country to raise the level of awareness of Brazilian society.	Cyber Security Culture
No Adherence	BR-22	Get to know, through PR, the critical information infrastructures of the APF bodies located outside the MD;	Cyber Security Culture
SOUTHERN AFRICADOS			
No Adherence	ZA-05	[CSIRTs] Create and maintain situational awareness of risk in South African cyberspace	Cyber Security Culture
No Adherence	ZA-06	[CSIRTs] Initiate national cybersecurity awareness campaigns	Cyber Security Culture
No Adherence	ZA-07	Participate in regional, African Union and international forums on issues pertaining to cyber security to ensure South Africa's foresight in defining and drawing up a global cyber security agenda to combat cyber crime and build secure and reliable information technology centres.	Cyber Security Culture
Adherence	ZA-08	Establishing bilateral and multilateral partnerships of national interest with various instruments such as memoranda of understanding, conventions and treaties.	Cyber Security Culture
Adherence	ZA-09	[NCSPF] Promote capacity building and research on a cyber security agenda and enhancement with South African Universities, industry and the Department of Science and Technology.	Cyber Security Culture
Adherence	ZA-10	[NCSPF] Implement cyber security awareness programmes for private sector, public sector and civil society users.	Cyber Security Culture
Adherence	ZA-11	[NCSPF] Encourage companies to develop a culture of cyber security,	Cyber Security Culture
Adherence	ZA-12	[NCSPF] Support outreach to civil society, children and individual users,	Cyber Security Culture
Adherence	ZA-13	[NCSPF] Promote a comprehensive national awareness programme and guidelines	Cyber Security Culture
No Adherence	ZA-14	[NCSPF] Review and update existing privacy regime,	Cyber Security Culture
Adherence	ZA-15	[NCSPF] Develop awareness of cyber risks and available solutions	Cyber Security Culture

Table 10- Comparison of Cybersecurity Culture in Brazil and India

ADHERENCE	CODE	GUIDELINES	CATEGORY
BRAZIL			
No Adherence	BR-17	Encourage the development and exchange of theses, dissertations and other similar works, with a doctrinal focus, in civilian and military higher education institutions of interest to St Cyber's activities;	Cyber Security Culture
Adherence IN-03	BR-18	Promote doctrinal, normative and technical exchanges with civilian and military institutions, both national and from friendly nations;	Cyber Security Culture
No Adherence	BR-19	Prospecting the needs of St Kitts and Nevis in the area of S,T&I, within the scope of defence, in order to identify the scientific and technological capacities needed to develop the sector;	Cyber Security Culture
No Adherence	BR-20	Identify specific competences (individual and organisational) in S,T&I, of interest to St Cyber, within the scope of the MD and civilian research and development centres (public and private), establishing partnerships between centres of excellence, at a national level, to aggregate institutions and avoid the dispersion of resources;	Cyber Security Culture
Adherence IN-05	BR-21	Propose to the federal government that a national education campaign on cyber defence be carried out, with the aim of mobilising the country to raise awareness among Brazilian society.	Cyber Security Culture
Adherence IN-04	BR-22	To know, through the PR, the critical information infrastructures of the APF bodies located outside the MD;	Cyber Security Culture
INDIA			
Adherence	IN-03	Enunciating the national information security policy and coordinating all aspects of information security governance in the country.	Cyber Security Culture
Adherence	IN-04	Creating the necessary situational awareness of threats to ICT infrastructure in order to determine and implement an appropriate response.	Cyber Security Culture
Adherence	IN-05	Creating a cybersecurity culture of responsible user behaviour and actions.	Cyber Security Culture

Table 11 - Comparison of Cyber Security Culture in Brazil and the United Kingdom

ADHERENCE	CODE	GUIDELINES	CATEGORY
BRAZIL			
Adhesion GB-13	BR-17	Encourage the development and exchange of theses, dissertations and other similar works, with a doctrinal focus, in civilian and military higher education institutions of interest to St Cyber's activities;	Cyber Security Culture
No Adherence	BR-18	Promote doctrinal, normative and technical exchanges with civilian and military institutions, both national and from friendly nations;	Cyber Security Culture
Adherence GB-17 and 18	BR-19	Prospecting the needs of St Kitts and Nevis in the area of S,T&I, within the scope of defence, in order to identify the scientific and technological capacities needed to develop the sector;	Cyber Security Culture
Partial Adhesion GB-19	BR-20	Identify specific competences (individual and organisational) in S,T&I, of interest to St Cyber, within the scope of the MD and civilian research and development centres (public and private), establishing partnerships between centres of excellence, at national level, to aggregate institutions and avoid the dispersion of resources;	Cyber Security Culture
Adhesion GB-12, 14 and 20	BR-21	Propose to the federal government that a national education campaign on cyber defence be carried out, with the aim of mobilising the country to raise the level of awareness of Brazilian society.	Cyber Security Culture
No Adherence	BR-22	To know, through the PR, the critical information infrastructures of the APF bodies located outside the MD;	Cyber Security Culture
UNITED KINGDOM			
Adherence	GB-12	Fostering a vibrant and innovative cybersecurity private sector to share information about threats in cyberspace	Cyber Security Culture
Adherence	GB-13	Encourage, support and develop education at all levels, essential key competences and R&D.	Cyber Security Culture
Adherence	GB-14	To help mould an open, cyberspace-stable and vibrant society that the UK public can use safely and that supports open societies.	Cyber Security Culture
Non-adherence	GB-15	Show tolerance and respect for diversity of language, culture and ideas	Cyber Security Culture
Non-adherence	GB-16	We will use cyber-relevant sanctions to combat cyber-crimes, such as online bullying or Internet fraud.	Cyber Security Culture
Adherence	GB-17	Working to raise awareness and to educate and empower people and companies to protect themselves online	Cyber Security Culture
Adherence	GB-18	Provide clear cyber security advice for use by anyone using the internet so that people can decide how they want to use cyberspace, informed about the risks	Cyber Security Culture
Partial Adherence	GB-19	Improving the information available to people buying safety products by encouraging the development of safety kitemarks. BIS works with domestic, European and global trade standards organisations.	Cyber Security Culture
Adherence	GB-20	Sensitise businesses to the threat and the actions they can take to protect themselves, including working across sectors of strategic importance to raise cyber security issues along their supply chains.	Cyber Security Culture

Table 12- Comparison of Security Infrastructure in Brazil and the United Kingdom

ADHERENCE	CODE	GUIDELINES	CATEGORY
Adhesion GB-25	BR-23	Create cyber intelligence structures, as required by the central intelligence bodies of the dasfa and the SMDC, to apply scientific and systematic methods, seeking to extract and analyse data from the cyber source, producing knowledge of interest;	Security infrastructure
UNITED KINGDOM			
NoAderence	GB-20	Sensitise businesses to the threat and the actions they can take to protect themselves, including working across sectors of strategic importance to raise cyber security issues along their supply chains.	Cyber Security Culture
NoAderence	GB-21	Helping consumers respond to the cyber threats that will be the "new normal" by using social media to provide warnings about fraud or other online threats.	Security infrastructure
NoAderence	GB-22	Help people identify if their computers have been compromised and what they can do to resolve the compromise and protect themselves from future attacks	Security infrastructure
NoAderence	GB-23	Ensure that new national procedures for responding to cyber incidents (ensuring that essential services can be maintained or restored quickly) are fully tested, both within the UK and in exercises with international partners.	Security infrastructure
NoAderence	GB-24	Build and maintain secure government ICT networks.	Security infrastructure
Adherence	GB-25	Sharpen our ability to identify the nature and attribution of cyber attacks.	Security infrastructure

Table 13- Comparison of Interaction with other bodies and actors in Brazil and South Africa

ADHERENCE	CODE	GUIDELINES	CATEGORY
BRAZIL			
Adhesion ZA-27	BR-24	Establishing risk criteria inherent in information assets and managing them, reducing the risks to critical information infrastructures of interest to national defence to acceptable levels;	Interaction with other bodies and players
Adhesion ZA-22	BR-25	Include cyber defence in combat simulation exercises and joint operations;	Interaction with other bodies and players
Adhesion ZA-22	BR-26	Plan and execute the adaptation of science, technology and innovation (S,T&I) structures, integrating efforts between the FA to meet the needs of St Cyber;	Interaction with other bodies and players
Adhesion ZA-22	BR-27	Create a permanent defence committee, made up of representatives of the MD and invited guests from other ministries and development agencies, to intensify and explore new opportunities for cooperation in S,T&I in areas of interest to St Cyber;	Interaction with other bodies and players
SOUTH AFRICA			
NoAderence	ZA-21	[CNCSC] Act as the single point of contact on cybersecurity matters relevant to national security (national defence, national intelligence and cybercrime)	Interaction with other bodies and players
Adherence	ZA-22	[CNCSC] Facilitating the sharing of information and the exchange of technologies relevant to national security in cyberspace	Interaction with other bodies and players
NoAderence	ZA-23	[CNCSC] Facilitate interaction at both national and international level, including through international associations of organisations such	Interaction with other bodies and players

ADHESIONS1	CODE	GUIDELINES	CATEGORY
		as the Incident Response Forum and security teams (first), and develop a policy to inform such interaction (second).	
NoAderence	ZA-24	[CSIRTs] Disseminate relevant CSIRTs information to the NCSC or other sectors if necessary,	Interaction with other bodies and players
NoAderence	ZA-25	[CSIRTs] Act as a single point of contact for that specific sector on cybersecurity issues	Interaction with other bodies and players
NoAderence	ZA-26	[CSIRTs] Establish information exchange of processes and procedures with the CNCSC as part of South Africa's National Cyber Security Coordination.	Interaction with other bodies and players
Adherence	ZA-27	[CSIRTs] Facilitate the exchange of technology and information between the sectors involved	Interaction with other bodies and players
NoAderence	ZA-28	[NCII] Facilitate the public-private partnership for the implementation of a protection plan for critical information infrastructures	Interaction with other bodies and players

Table 14 - Comparison of interaction with other bodies and actors in Brazil and the United States

ADHESIONS1	CODE	GUIDELINES	CATEGORY
		BRAZIL	
US-19 grip	BR-24	Establishing risk criteria inherent in information assets and managing them, reducing the risks to critical information infrastructures of interest to national defence to acceptable levels;	Interaction with other bodies and players
No Adherence	BR-25	Include cyber defence in combat simulation exercises and joint operations;	Interaction with other bodies and players
US-21 and 22 grip	BR-26	Plan and execute the adaptation of science, technology and innovation (S,T&I) structures, integrating efforts between the FA to meet the needs of St Cyber;	Interaction with other bodies and players
Partial Adhesion US-23	BR-27	Create a permanent defence committee made up of representatives from the Ministry of Defence and invited guests from other ministries and development agencies, to intensify and explore new opportunities for cooperation in S,T&I in areas of interest to St Ciber;	Interaction with other bodies and players
		UNITED STATES	
No Adherence	US-16	Convene inter-agency mechanisms necessary to conduct interagency legal analyses of priority cybersecurity-related issues identified during the development policy formulation process and formulate coherent unified policy guidance that clarifies the roles, responsibilities, as well as the application of agency authorities for cybersecurity-related activities across the federal government.	Interaction with other bodies and players
No Adherence	US-17	Develop US government positions for an international cyber security policy framework and strengthen our international partnerships to create initiatives that embrace the full range of activities, policies and opportunities associated with cyber security.	Interaction with other bodies and players
No Adherence	US-18	Develop a process between the private sector, the government and help to prevent, detect and respond to cyber incidents.	Interaction with other bodies and players
Adherence	US-19	Expand information sharing on network incidents and vulnerabilities with allies and seek bilateral and multilateral agreements that will improve economic and security interests while protecting civil liberties and privacy rights.	Interaction with other bodies and players
No Adherence	US-20	Encourage collaboration between academic and industrial laboratories to develop path migration and incentives for the rapid adoption of technology development research and innovation.	Interaction with other bodies and players
Adherence	US-21	Leadership must be high and strongly anchored within the White House to guide, coordinate action and achieve results	Interaction with other bodies and players
Adherence	US-22	Clarification of the related cyber security roles and responsibilities of federal government departments and agencies, providing the policy, legal frameworks and necessary coordination to enable them to fulfil their missions.	Interaction with other bodies and players
Adherence	US-23	0 President should consider appointing a cybersecurity policy officer in the White House, who would report to the NSC and accumulate duties with the NEC, to coordinate the Nation's cybersecurity-related policies and activities. This individual would chair the ICI-IPC and lead a robust process in consultation with other EOP elements to resolve competing priorities and coordinate interagency cybersecurity policy and strategy development.	Interaction with other bodies and players

Table 15 - Comparison of interaction with other bodies and actors in Brazil and India

ADHERENCE	CODE	GUIDELINES	CATEGORY
		BRAZIL	
Adherence IN-08	BR-24	Establishing risk criteria inherent in information assets and managing them, reducing the risks to critical information infrastructures of interest to national defence to acceptable levels;	Interaction with other bodies and players
No Adherence	BR-25	Include cyber defence in combat simulation exercises and joint operations;	Interaction with other bodies and players
Adhesion IN-06	BR-26	Plan and execute the adaptation of science, technology and innovation (S,T&I) structures, integrating efforts between the FA to meet the needs of St Cyber;	Interaction with other bodies and players
Adhesion IN-06	BR-27	Create a permanent defence committee, made up of representatives from the MD and invited guests from other ministries and development agencies, to intensify and explore new opportunities for cooperation in S,T&I in areas of interest to St Cyber;	Interaction with other bodies and players
		INDIA	
Adherence	IN-06	Identifying national security organisations and coordinating matters related to information security in the country.	Interaction with other bodies and players
No Adherence	IN-07	Catalyse activities of strategic importance to the nation related to cyber defence	Interaction with other bodies and players
Adherence	IN-08	Expansion of the Cyber Warning and Information Network to support the government's role in coordinating crisis management for cyberspace security;	Interaction with other bodies and players

Table 16- Comparison of interaction with other bodies and actors in Brazil and the UK

ADHERENCE	CODE	GUIDELINES	CATEGORY
		BRAZIL	
No Adherence	BR-24	Establishing risk criteria inherent in information assets and managing them, reducing the risks to critical information infrastructures of interest to national defence to acceptable levels;	Interaction with other bodies and players
Adhesion GB-37	BR-25	Include cyber defence in combat simulation exercises and joint operations;	Interaction with other bodies and players
Adhesion GB-30	BR-26	Plan and execute the adaptation of science, technology and innovation (S,T&I) structures, integrating efforts between the FA to meet the needs of St Cyber;	Interaction with other bodies and players
GB-29 grip	BR-27	Create a permanent defence committee, made up of representatives of the MD and invited guests from other ministries and development agencies, to intensify and explore new opportunities for cooperation in S,T&I in areas of interest to St Cyber;	Interaction with other bodies and players
		UNITED KINGDOM	
No Adherence	GB-26	Establishing new operational partnerships with private sectors, building important information points in cyberspace	Interaction with other bodies and players
No Adherence	GB-27	Helping consumers respond to the cyber threats that will be the "new normal" by using the media to warn people about scams or other online threats.	Interaction with other bodies and players
No Adherence	GB-28	Working collectively to tackle the threat of criminals operating online.	Interaction with other bodies and players
Adherence	GB-29	Supporting the work of all four NCA operational commands (borders, organised crime, economic crime and Child Exploitation and Online Protection - CEOP) by providing specialist support, intelligence and guidance.	Interaction with other bodies and players
Adherence	GB-30	Support police forces across England and Wales to drive greater national capability on cybercrime, including through training law enforcement on cyber issues, and making sure links to related issues such as bullying or child exploitation are made.	Interaction with other bodies and players
No Adherence	GB-31	Ensure the best possible flow of information between police and ANC forces	Interaction with other bodies and players
No Adherence	GB-32	Supporting forces to move towards full reporting of online crime, helping them to identify good practices.	Interaction with other bodies and players
No Adherence	GB-33	Working with consumers, we need to raise awareness in the business of the potential threat to reputation, revenue and intellectual property from a cyber attack.	Interaction with other bodies and players
No Adherence	GB-34	Enable the UK's cyber security industry to thrive and expand, supporting it in accessing markets abroad.	Interaction with other bodies and players
No Adherence	GB-35	Encouraging industry-led standards and guidelines that are easily used and understood, and that help companies that are good at security make that a selling point.	Interaction with other bodies and players
No Adherence	GB-36	Working with allies to ensure the implementation of NATO's cyber defence policy	Interaction with other bodies and players
Adherence	GB-37	Creating and building a dedicated and integrated civilian and military capability within the Ministry of Defence. Cyber integration within the organisation and creation of a Defence.	Interaction with other bodies and players
No Adherence	GB-38	Strengthen international systems to build trust between states in cyberspace, including through engagement within the OSCE on confidence-building measures.	Interaction with other bodies and players

Table 17- Comparison of Standardisation in Brazil and South Africa

ADHESIONS1	CODE	GUIDELINES	CATEGORY
		BRAZIL	
No Adherence	BR-28	Define the profiles of the staff needed to carry out St Cyber's activities;	Standardisation
No Adherence	BR-29	Create specific positions and functions and staff them with specialised personnel to meet St Ciber's needs;	Standardisation
No Adherence	BR-30	Establish criteria and control the mobilisation and demobilisation of personnel for cyber defence activities;	Standardisation
Adhesion US-26 and 28	BR-31	To create and standardise cyber security processes in order to standardise accreditation procedures within the scope of critical information infrastructures of interest to national defence; and to establish programmes/projects in order to ensure the capacity to act securely on the network, thereby strengthening the operability of the MD's command and control (c2) activity.	Standardisation
No Adherence	BR-32	Create the cyber defence doctrine at the proposal of the SMDC central body;	Standardisation
US-25 grip	BR-33	Designate the central body of the SMDC as responsible for proposing innovations and doctrinal updates for St Cyber within the defence framework.	Standardisation
No Adherence	BR-34	To implement a defence CIS management methodology, taking into account current legislation and standards, best	Standardisation

		practices, defence intelligence doctrine and international standards of interest;	
US-29 and 30 grip	BR-35	Keeping the cyber defence policy up to date in line with the national cyber security policy, when it exists;	Standardisation
No Adherence	BR-36	Defining roles and responsibilities for carrying out activities related to cyber defence;	Standardisation
US-27 grip	BR-37	Drawing up proposals for the creation and adaptation of federal legislation to support cyber defence activities;	Standardisation
No Adherence	BR-38	Propose the creation of a budget programme to make St Ciber's actions and activities viable;	Standardisation
No Adherence	BR-39	Proposing the adaptation of the national mobilisation law and the national mobilisation system to make them compatible with the needs of St Ciber.	Standardisation
No Adherence	BR-40	Draw up mobilisation plans for information assets, with the respective costs, in line with the national mobilisation law;	Standardisation
No Adherence	BR-41	Adapt the SMDC's mobilisation requirements standards to SINAMOB; and	Standardisation
		SOUTH AFRICA	
No Adherence	US-24	Designate cyber security as one of the President's main management priorities and establish performance metrics.	Standardisation
Adherence	US-25	Designate an official privacy and civil liberties body for the cybersecurity directorate of the NSC.	Standardisation
Adherence	US-26	Prepare a cyber security incident response plan and start a dialogue to improve public-private partnerships with an eye to rationalisation, aligning and offering resources to optimise their contribution and engagement.	Standardisation
Adherence	US-27	Improve the resolution process between agencies on interpretations of the law and enforcement of policy and the authorities for cyber operations.	Standardisation
Adherence	US-28	Use the infrastructure objectives and research and development framework to set targets for national and international organisations.	Standardisation
Adherence	US-29	The official cybersecurity policy must be involved in all economic measures, counter-terrorism, science and technology policies and decisions to inform them from a cybersecurity perspective.	Standardisation
Adherence	US-30	The president's policy must have clear presidential support, sufficient authority and resources to operate effectively in the formulation of policies and the coordination of activities related to cyber security in the interagency.	Standardisation
No Adherence	US-31	The official cyber security policy must be supported by at least two Directors General and appropriate NSC staff, and of course at least one Senior Director together with NEC staff.	Standardisation
No Adherence	US-32	The official cyber security policy should not have the operational responsibility or authority to make policy unilaterally	Standardisation

Table 18- Comparison of standardisation in Brazil and India

ADHERENCE			CATEGORY
		BRAZIL	
No Adherence	BR-28	Define the profiles of the staff needed to carry out St Cyber's activities;	Standardisation
No Adherence	BR-29	Create specific positions and functions and staff them with specialised personnel to meet St Ciber's needs;	Standardisation
No Adherence	BR-30	Establish criteria and control the mobilisation and demobilisation of personnel for cyber defence activities;	Standardisation
Partial Adherence IN-10	BR-31	To create and standardise cyber security processes in order to standardise accreditation procedures within the scope of critical information infrastructures of interest to national defence; and to establish programmes/projects in order to ensure the capacity to act securely on the network, thereby strengthening the operability of the MD's command and control (c2) activity.	Standardisation
No Adherence	BR-32	Create the cyber defence doctrine at the proposal of the SMDC central body;	Standardisation
No Adherence	BR-33	Designate the central body of the SMDC as responsible for proposing innovations and doctrinal updates for St Cyber within the defence framework.	Standardisation
No Adherence	BR-34	To implement a defence CIS management methodology, taking into account current legislation and standards, best practices, defence intelligence doctrine and international standards of interest;	Standardisation
Adherence IN-09	BR-35	Keeping the cyber defence policy up to date in line with the national cyber security policy, when it exists;	Standardisation
No Adherence	BR-36	Defining roles and responsibilities for carrying out activities related to cyber defence;	Standardisation
No Adherence	BR-37	Drawing up proposals for the creation and adaptation of federal legislation to support cyber defence activities;	Standardisation
No Adherence	BR-38	Propose the creation of a budget programme to make St Ciber's actions and activities viable;	Standardisation
No Adherence	BR-39	Proposing the adaptation of the national mobilisation law and the national mobilisation system to make them compatible with the needs of St Ciber.	Standardisation
No Adherence	BR-40	Draw up mobilisation plans for information assets, with the respective costs, in line with the national mobilisation law;	Standardisation
No Adherence	BR-41	Adapting the rules for SMDC mobilisation needs to SINAMOB; and	Standardisation
		INDIA	
Adherence	IN-09	Implementing the organisation's security policies in line with international standards.	Standardisation
Adherence	IN-10	Develop a comprehensive maintenance and repair policy to increase the availability of cyber resources for all users in an efficient manner.	Standardisation
No Adherence	IN-11	Creating a favourable legal environment in favour of safe cyberspace, adequate trust and confidence in electronic transactions, increased law enforcement resources that can enable responsible action by stakeholders and effective prosecution.	Standardisation
No Adherence	IN-12	Political actions, promotion that enable compliance with international safety best practices and conformity assessment (product, process, technology and people) and Incentives for compliance.	Standardisation

Table 19 - Comparison of standardisation in Brazil and the UK

ADHERENCE	CODE	GUIDELINES	CATEGORY
No Adherence	BR-28	Define the profiles of the staff needed to carry out St Cyber's activities;	Standardisation
No Adherence	BR-29	Create specific posts and functions and staff them with specialised personnel to meet St Ciber's needs;	Standardisation
No Adherence	BR-30	Establish criteria and control the mobilisation and demobilisation of personnel for cyber defence activities;	Standardisation
No Adherence	BR-31	To create and standardise cyber security processes in order to standardise accreditation procedures within the scope of critical information infrastructures of interest to national defence; and to establish programmes/projects in order to ensure the capacity to act securely on the network, thus strengthening the operability of the command and control (c2) activity in the MD.	Standardisation
Adhesion GB-48	BR-32	Create the cyber defence doctrine at the proposal of the SMDC central body;	Standardisation
No Adherence	BR-33	Designate the central body of the SMDC as responsible for proposing innovations and doctrinal updates for St Cyber within the defence framework.	Standardisation
GB-43 grip	BR-34	Implement a defence CIS management methodology, taking into account current legislation and standards, best practices, defence intelligence doctrine and international standards of interest;	Standardisation
Partial Adhesion GB-50	BR-35	Keeping the cyber defence policy up to date in line with the national cyber security policy, when it exists;	Standardisation
No Adherence	BR-35	Defining roles and responsibilities for carrying out activities related to cyber defence;	Standardisation
GB-44 grip	BR-37	Drawing up proposals for the creation and adaptation of federal legislation to support cyber defence activities;	Standardisation
No Adherence	BR-38	Propose the creation of a budget programme to make St Ciber's actions and activities viable;	Standardisation
No Adherence	BR-39	Proposing the adaptation of the national mobilisation law and the national mobilisation system to make them compatible with the needs of St Ciber.	Standardisation
No Adherence	BR-40	Draw up mobilisation plans for information assets, with the respective costs, in line with the national mobilisation law;	Standardisation
No Adherence	BR-41	Adapt the SMDC's mobilisation requirements standards to SINAMOB; and	Standardisation
No Adherence	GB-39	Incentivise industry-led standards and guidelines	Standardisation
No Adherence	GB-40	Create specific law to give cybercrime investigation capacity to the new National Crime Agency	Standardisation
No Adherence	GB-41	Encourage the use of "cyber-specialists" to make more use of those with specialised skills to help the police.	Standardisation
No Adherence	GB-42	Make sure we can co-operate in law enforcement and deny refuge to cyber criminals.	Standardisation
Adherence	GB-43	Modelling cybersecurity best practices on the government's own systems, setting strong standards for government suppliers to ensure that the bar is raised.	Standardisation
Adherence	GB-44	Ensuring the UK has a solid legal framework that allows law enforcement agencies to combat cybercrime.	Standardisation
No Adherence	GB-45	Work to ensure that law enforcement agencies and the judiciary are aware of the additional powers the courts already have to protect the public when there is great reason to believe that someone may commit more serious cyberorimes.	Standardisation
No Adherence	GB-46	Include restrictions on the use of the internet are used to protect the public or victims in cases of sexual crimes, harassment and anti-social behaviour, through guidance that will encourage the judicial system to consider such cyber-relevant sanctions for cyber offences where appropriate.	Standardisation
No Adherence	GB-47	Impulse work on the design of online crime, development of best security practices, and effective crime prevention advice for all levels of business.	Standardisation
No Adherence	GB-48	Take steps to make sure it is simple and straightforward for members of the public to report cybercrime, of course this should include the possibility of doing so online.	Standardisation
No Adherence	GB-49	Looking at the best ways to improve cyber security education at all levels so that people are better equipped to use cyberspace safely.	Standardisation
Partial adhesion GB-43	GB-50	Stimulating the development of industry-led standards and guidance that help customers navigate the market and differentiate companies with adequate levels of protection and good cyber security products.	Standardisation

Table 20 - Comparison of Information Security in Brazil and South Africa

ADHERENCE	CODE	GUIDELINES	CATEGORY
Adhesion ZA-38	BR-42	Designing and implementing the military cyber defence system (SMDC), with the participation of AF military personnel and civilians;	Information Security
Adhesion ZA-38	BR-43	Create a structure to coordinate and integrate St Cyber within the MD, as the central body of the SMDC, with the possibility of military and civilian participation;	Information Security
Adhesion ZA-41	BR-44	surveying critical information infrastructures associated with internal and external threats, real or potential, to contribute to the formation of the situational awareness necessary for intelligence activities.	Information Security
No Adherence	BR-45	Create a knowledge management system of lessons learnt to compose and update the doctrine, and	Information Security
No Adherence	BR-46	Implementing a defence public key infrastructure (icp defence);	Information Security
No Adherence	BR-47	Determine interoperable defence cryptography standards in addition to those of the FA; and implement the defence sic audit system.	Information Security
Adhesion ZA-43	BR-48	Revising the planning of employment hypotheses to take account of actions in cyberspace; and	Information Security
No Adherence	BR-49	Carry out a systematic survey of information assets that can be mobilised for St Cyber;	Information Security
No Adherence	BR-50	Draw up and keep up to date a database of information assets of interest to the mobilisation in favour of the SMDC;	Information Security
Adherence	ZA-38	The Crime Prevention and Security Justice body, with the help of other government bodies, will implement the cyber security policy to ensure centralised coordination.	Information Security
No Adherence	ZA-39	A Cybersecurity Response Committee chaired by the State Security Agency will be established within the Crime Prevention and Security Justice body to coordinate cybersecurity activities.	Information Security
No Adherence	ZA-40	The National Cyber Security Coordination Centre (CNCSC), which will be established by the PCJS, will play a supervisory and coordinating role in operations in all the Security Incident Response Groups.	Information Security
Adherence	ZA-41	The CNCSC will provide national guidelines and standards on the establishment of CSIRTs with a special focus on national security issues.	Information Security
No Adherence	ZA-42	CNCSC] Perform any other function associated with this objective.	Information Security
Adherence	ZA-43	CSIRTs] Conduct cybersecurity readiness audits, assessments and exercises for the sector	Information Security
No Adherence	ZA-44	NCSPF] To promote the capacity to develop South African strategies in specific skills to meet the growing challenges of dealing with cyber security threats.	Information Security
No Adherence	ZA-45	NCSPF] Promote the capacity to recruit and retain strategists in order to ensure the technical level for the development of the republic's cyber security needs.	Information Security
No Adherence	ZA-45	NCSPF] Promote the development and/or adoption of South African standards and international standards bodies to secure cyberspace and thus leverage e-commerce and the information society.	Information Security

Table 21- Comparison of Information Security in Brazil and the United States

ADHERENCE	ID	BRAZIL	CATEGORY
US-34 grip	BR-42	Design and implement the military cyber defence system (SMDC), with the participation of AF military personnel and civilians;	Information Security
US-33 grip	BR 43	Create a structure to coordinate and integrate St Cyber within the MD, as the central body of the SMDC, with the possibility of the participation of Military of the FA and civilians;	Information Security
US-35 grip	BR 44	Survey critical information infrastructures associated with internal and external threats, real or potential, to help build the situational awareness needed for intelligence activities.	Information Security
US-40 grip	BR-45	Create a knowledge management system of lessons learnt to compose and update doctrine, and	Information Security
No Adherence	BR-46	Implement a defence public key infrastructure (icp defence);	Information Security
No Adherence	BR-47	Determine interoperable defence cryptography standards in addition to those of the FA; and implement the defence sic audit system.	Information Security
US-35 grip	BR-48	Revise the planning of employment hypotheses to take account of actions in cyberspace; and	Information Security
US-37 grip	BR-49	Carry out a systematic survey of information assets that can be mobilised for St Cyber;	Information Security
US-43 grip	BR-50	Draw up and keep up to date a database of information assets of interest to the mobilisation in favour of the SMDC;	Information Security
No Adherence	US-32	The official cyber security policy should not have the operational responsibility or authority to make policy unilaterally	Standardisation
Adherence	US-33	Appoint a body in accordance with the cyber security policy responsible for coordinating the nation's policies and activities.	Information Security
Adherence	US-34	Establishing a strong relationship, under the direction of the cybersecurity policy officer, it will accumulate functions with the NSC and the NEC, to coordinate the inter-institutional development of cybersecurity-related strategy and policy.	Information Security
Adherence	US-35	To protect the information and communications infrastructure, this strategy must include the continuous evaluation of activities at the NCIC and, where necessary, building on its successes.	Information Security
Adherence	US-36	Develop a framework for research and development of strategies that technologies have the potential to increase the focus on the game-changing security, reliability, resilience and dependability of digital infrastructure;	Information Security
Adherence	US-37	Provide research into event data to facilitate the development of tools, test community theories and identify viable solutions.	Information Security
No Adherence	US-38	Use OMB's programme evaluation framework to ensure that departments and agencies use performance-based budgeting in pursuit of cyber security objectives.	Information Security
No Adherence	US-39	Develop a set of threat scenarios and metrics that can be used for risk management decisions, recovery planning and S&T prioritisation.	Information Security
No Adherence	US-40	Develop mechanisms for sharing information related to cyber security that respond to concerns about privacy and confidential information and make information sharing mutually beneficial.	Information Security
No Adherence	US-41	Developing solutions for emergency communications resources during a period of natural disaster, crisis or conflict, guaranteeing net neutrality.	Information Security
No Adherence	US-42	Implementing high-value activities (e.g. the Smart Grid), an opt-in identity matrix and interoperable management systems to build trust for online transactions and to improve privacy.	Information Security
Adherence	US-43	Improve government procurement strategies and market incentives for flexible hardware and software insurance, security innovations, and secure management services.	Information Security
No Adherence	US-44	Having the responsibility to protect and defend the country, and all levels of government have the responsibility to guarantee the security and well-being of citizens.	Information Security
No Adherence	US-45	The regional and functional directorate must designate a person to be responsible for monitoring issues related to cybersecurity in the directorate's portfolio and coordinating with the cybersecurity directorate.	Information Security
No Adherence	US-46	The national strategy must focus senior leadership attention and time on resolving the issues that hamper US efforts to achieve reliable, resilient global information security factors and related communications infrastructure and technological capabilities	Information Security

Table 22 - Comparison of Information Security in Brazil and India

ADHERENCE	ID	Description	CATEGORY
BRAZIL			
No Adherence	BR-42	Designing and implementing the military cyber defence system (SMDC), with the participation of AF military personnel and civilians;	Information Security
Adhesion IN-37	BR-43	Create a structure to coordinate and integrate St Cyber within the MD, as the central body of the SMDC, with the possibility of military and civilian participation;	Information Security
Adhesion IN-34	BR-44	To survey critical information infrastructures associated with real or potential internal and external threats, in order to help build the situational awareness necessary for intelligence activities.	Information Security
Adhesion IN-35	BR-45	Create a knowledge management system of lessons learnt to compose and update the doctrine; and	Information Security
No Adherence	BR-46	Implement a defence public key infrastructure (icp defence);	Information Security
No Adherence	BR-47	Determine interoperable defence cryptography standards in addition to those of the FA; and implement the defence sic audit system.	Information Security
Adhesion IN-14	BR-48	Revising the planning of employment hypotheses to take account of actions in cyberspace; and	Information Security
Adhesion IN-13	BR-49	Carry out a systematic survey of information assets that can be mobilised for St Cyber;	Information Security
Partial Adherence IN-18	BR-50	Draw up and keep up to date a database of information assets of interest to the mobilisation in favour of the SMDC;	Information Security
INDIA			
Adherence	IN-13	Identify and classify critical information infrastructure facilities and assets.	Information Security
Adherence	IN-14	Implement national security threat and vulnerability assessments to understand the real consequences	Information Security
No Adherence	IN-15	Law enforcement, information security incident handling and crisis management processes on a 24x7 basis.	Information Security
No Adherence	IN-16	Preparing and managing emergency communication crises, redundancy and disaster recovery plans, testing and evaluating plans, etc.	Information Security
No Adherence	IN-17	Periodically checking the levels of preparedness for critical information infrastructure emergencies and the recovery time in the event of cyber attacks.	Information Security
Partial Adherence	IN-18	Implementation of a system to contain, eradicate and recover data.	Information Security
No Adherence	IN-19	Carry out information infrastructure audits on an annual basis, independent of IT security and the audit organisation.	Information Security
No Adherence	IN-20	Implement in accordance with the best international practices for security, quality of service and service level in accordance with the (SLAs) and demonstration.	Information Security
No Adherence	IN-21	Use safe products and services and skilled labour to keep crisis management and emergency response in line.	Information Security
No Adherence	IN-22	Use legal software and update at regular intervals.	Information Security
No Adherence	IN-23	Watch out for security traps, while adhering to security alerts on the Internet.	Information Security
No Adherence	IN-24	Ensuring the security of cyberspace, using the appropriate technology and, most importantly, involving the right types of people with the right awareness, ethics and behaviour.	Information Security
	IN-25	Protection of IT and critical information and communication networks and gateways.	Information Security
No Adherence	IN-26	Putting in place a 24 x 7 cyber security mechanism for emergency response and resolution and crisis management through effective forecasting, prevention, protection, response and recovery actions.	Information Security
No Adherence	IN-27	Indian development of techniques and technology through appropriate security boundary technology research, solution orientated research, proof of concept, pilot development and deployment of IT product/process security.	Information Security
No Adherence	IN-28	Carry out effective cyber crime prevention and prosecutorial actions.	Information Security
No Adherence	IN-29	Provide proactive preventive and reactive mitigation actions to reach and neutralise the sources of problems and support the creation of a global security eco-system, including public-private partnerships, information sharing, bilateral and multi-lateral agreements with overseas CERTs, security agencies and security companies etc.	Information Security
No Adherence	IN-30	Carry out data protection while processing, handling, storing and transporting and protecting sensitive personal information to create the necessary environment of trust.	Information Security
No Adherence	IN-31	Identify the most dangerous classes of cyber security threats to the nation, in IT analyse the most critical of infrastructure vulnerabilities, and the most difficult security problems in the cyber sphere.	Information Security
No Adherence	IN-32	Strengthen the capacity of critical ICT infrastructure to resist cyber attacks.	Information Security
No Adherence	IN-33	Minimise damage and recover in a reasonable timeframe.	Information Security
Adherence	IN-34	Apply cybersecurity in IT training and exercises and business continuity depends on critical sector plans to assess the level of emergency preparedness of critical information infrastructures in resisting cyber attacks and minimising damage and recovery time in the event of cyber attacks occurring.	Information Security
Adherence	IN-35	Carry out analysis, surveillance and alert activities, enable the exchange of information and facilitate restoration efforts.	Information Security
No Adherence	IN-36	Provide regular updates to senior management on the progress of the incident handling process.	Information Security
Adherence	IN-37	Coordinate efforts to protect the country's critical information infrastructure and enable the development of skills in communication, interception, monitoring and early warning and vulnerability checks with the appropriate authorisation.	Information Security

Table 23 - Comparison of Information Security in Brazil and the United Kingdom

ADHERENCE	ID	Description	CATEGORY
BRAZIL			
No Adherence	BR-42	Designing and implementing the military cyber defence system (SMDC), with the participation of AF military personnel and civilians;	Information Security
No Adherence	BR-43	Create a structure to coordinate and integrate St Cyber within the MD, as the central body of the SMDC, with the possibility of military and civilian participation;	Information Security
GB-77 grip	BR-44	Survey critical information infrastructures associated with internal and external threats, real or potential, to help build the situational awareness necessary for intelligence activities.	Information Security
Partial Adhesion GB-78	BR-45	Create a knowledge management system of lessons learnt to compose and update the doctrine; and	Information Security
Partial Adhesion GB-79	BR-46	Implement a defence public key infrastructure (icp defence);	Information Security
No Adherence	BR-47	Determine interoperable defence cryptography standards in addition to those of the FA; and implement the defence sic audit system.	Information Security
No Adherence	BR-48	Revising the planning of employment hypotheses to take account of actions in cyberspace; and	Information Security
No Adherence	BR-49	Carry out a systematic survey of information assets that can be mobilised for St Cyber;	Information Security
No Adherence	BR-50	Draw up and keep up to date a database of information assets of interest to the mobilisation in favour of the SMDC;	Information Security
UNITED KINGDOM			
No Adherence	GB-51	Helping consumers and small businesses navigate the market by encouraging the development of clear indicators of good cyber security products.	Information Security
No Adherence	GB-52	Carry out a professional strategy in business services, including insurers, auditors, and lawyers to determine the role they can play in promoting better cyber risk management.	Information Security
No Adherence	GB-53	Build an effective, easy-to-use, simple point to report cyber fraud and improve the police response at a local level for those who are victims of cyber crime	Information Security
No Adherence	GB-54	Fight cybercrime and be one of the safest places in the world to do business in cyberspace	Information Security
No Adherence	GB-55	To be more resistant to cyber attacks and better able to protect our interests in cyberspace.	Information Security
No Adherence	GB-56	Act proportionately in cyberspace, and in accordance with national legislation and international law	Information Security
No Adherence	GB-57	Ensuring that cyberspace remains open to innovation and the free circulation of ideas, information and expression.	Information Security
No Adherence	GB-58	Respect individual privacy rights and provide adequate protection for intellectual property.	Information Security
No Adherence	GB-59	Creation of a competitive environment that guarantees a fair return on investment in networks, services and content.	Information Security
No Adherence	GB-60	Improve our ability to defend against and deter high-end, state-sponsored threats, and to prevent these techniques becoming available to non-state actors.	Information Security
No Adherence	GB-61	Maintain an effective framework and enforcement capabilities to disrupt and prosecute cybercrime.	Information Security
No Adherence	GB-62	Ensuring that information intelligence is fed back into effective action and advice for the public.	Information Security
No Adherence	GB-63	Carry out underlying research and development to maintain the production of innovative solutions.	Information Security
No Adherence	GB-64	Creating a thriving market in cyber security products and services that can win the UK business abroad and contribute to growth.	Information Security
No Adherence	GB-65	Look closely at how intelligence (for example, on threats to children provided by CEOP) is used by forces and how the result of the action of the forces and the courts is fed back to develop the best possible picture on threats.	Information Security
No Adherence	GB-66	Provide facilities for the public to report crime online, although these range from basic systems for certain types of crime to fully integrated crime reporting tools.	Information Security
No Adherence	GB-67	Report fraud, including cyber fraud, via the internet using the Fraud Action tool.	Information Security
No Adherence	GB-68	Building our intelligence framework through the National Fraud Intelligence Bureau, improving the targeting of enforcement resources and feeding into crime prevention councils.	Information Security
No Adherence	GB-69	Finding ways to improve the profile and transparency of information on cyber security breaches.	Information Security
No Adherence	GB-70	Explore ways in which industry-led standards for companies' cyber security performance can be used as a general market differentiator	Information Security
No Adherence	GB-71	Review existing legislation, for example the Computer Misuse Act 1990, to ensure that it remains relevant and effective.	Information Security
No Adherence	GB-72	To explore ways in which GCHQ's expertise could more directly benefit economic growth and support the development of the UK's cyber security sector without compromising the security of the agency's core and intelligence mission.	Information Security
No Adherence	GB-73	Promote robust levels of cybersecurity in online public services, enabling people to transact online with the government with confidence.	Information Security
No Adherence	GB-74	Develop a better understanding of the cyber security industry's strengths, potential growth and barriers to success.	Information Security
No Adherence	GB-75	Develop a marketing strategy to promote the UK's cyber security capabilities internationally	Information Security
No Adherence	GB-76	Expand the government council to include a wide range of organisations whose resilience is a priority for the UK economy.	Information Security
Adherence	GB-77	Maintaining and strengthening our ability to anticipate, prepare for and disrupt hostile acts in cyberspace (including improving information exchange across government and industry partners, improving defence against hostile acts and increasing law enforcement capacity to investigate and punish those who carry out hostile acts).	Information Security
Partial Adherence	GB-78	Maintain the capabilities that allow the Kingdom freedom of action and cyber advantage and preserve our sovereign capabilities in niche areas.	Information Security

APPENDIX 7

1. Based on your experience, how is Brazil's Cyber Defence Policy viewed by foreign countries, local and international institutions?

2. What is your perception of the approach to the PCD by the Brazilian APF?

3. Do you think there are issues addressed in other cyber security policies that would be relevant to Brazilian policy? What would these issues be?

4. According to your experience, is there any guideline addressed in Brazilian politics that shouldn't be included in its composition?

5. As an expert on the subject, how do you see the guidelines for directly combating cyber-terrorism and cyber-crime aimed at guaranteeing the security of local actors such as companies and civilians?

6. How can respect for an individual's right to privacy be addressed by a cyber security policy?

7. What is your view on the inclusion of cyber defence in combat simulation exercises and joint operations, including other agencies of the APF?

8. According to your knowledge, is the creation and maintenance of situational awareness about risk in cyberspace as a guideline for a country's Cyber Security Policy relevant to the creation of a Cyber Security Culture?

9. One of the guidelines of the Brazilian PCD is the identification of both individual and organisational competences, seeking partnerships in order to exchange experiences in the cyber sector. Is this action important for the development of Brazil's APF cyber sector? Are there any risks involved in involving private or civil partners?

10. Do you think international co-operation is important for the development of cyber security? For what reason?

11. What is your view on the lack of international co-operation in the Brazilian PCD guidelines?

12. Is the training of specialised technical personnel in the cyber sector important for the development of a knowledge framework for the APF?

13. Based on your experience, for better coordination on the subject of cyber security, should the sectors responsible for coordinating cyber security and cyber defence be subordinated directly to a responsible body/sector?

APPENDIX 8

Alcyon: The interview is quite...

Speaker: Why are you calling it Brazil's Cyber Policy?!

Speaker: Cyber defence policy

Alcyon: Maybe I put the acronym backwards and I'm trying to adjust it... sorry.

Speaker: I'm telling you this because there's already a division between cyber security and cyber defence...this is information and communications security for me, and here there's another note on paper, equipment, people. Cyber defence is just one part of information and communications security, this is law as the Brazilian legislation is written.

Speaker: Come on

Alcyon: Exactly

Alcyon: According to the information, I began to look at the policies that exist in the United Kingdom that are published and I began to have some adherences. So I raised some questions. So I'll ask you the first question.

Alcyon: Based on your experience, how is cyber defence policy seen in Brazil, by foreign countries, local and international institutions, since you go to conferences a lot, what do they say about us like that?

Speaker: As I said, the agent has a vision that cyber defence is not the only thing we have.

Vulnerability operates in the field of cyber security, and the actors are: federal police, slti, serpro, agent, there are a number of actors when looking at vulnerabilities.

Threats, roughly speaking...what comes from outside is the ministry of defence, specifically the army, and it has this preponderance, which I don't agree with, I think it should be the defence and not the army, it should be the whole defence, despite everything that is being put together, it is the defence.

The preponderance is still with the army, and I think it has to be with all defence.

And I can't understand defence doing it, Rio plus 20, Confederations Cup, it's doing it because it doesn't have a vision of a country that this has to be organised outside of there, it has to be organised in another sphere, because the map we have isn't cyber defence, it's more cyber security, it's vulnerabilities, it's attacks, it's day-to-day life, it's political structures that aren't necessarily organic defence and the defence of infrastructure, and expensive software and specialists, that's not in the field of cyber defence.

So when we talk about cyber defence, the military in other countries understand that our defence is very well designed. When you talk to international organisations about cyber defence, people stare and say that there's another piece missing... and they do.

I'll give you an example of my own.

The American government was very much in favour of cyber defence, cyber security, critical infrastructure protection... there's a whole series of things like that, filing their cyber security project, the 40 days of cyber security, and it was their first work in this area, it was even Melissa Hathaway who did it, a fantastic piece of work, and then suddenly the Americans started talking about electronic, cyber crime.

And I had this thought in my head, I didn't really understand it and I spoke to Melissa, who is a personal friend of mine...explain something to me, you were giving everyone a hard time about cyber-terrorism, cyber-attacks...dust!!! why a crime?

Melissa: Speak to the speaker: How many attacks do you receive every day in Brazil? Speaker: Thousands!

Melissa: And China?

Speaker: Thousands minus 10 to 1...I don't know!!!

Melissa: Yes, this is the same problem we have here in the United States, now an attack by one country on another is war, and I can't declare war on China 2,000 times a day, so if I turn these cyber issues into crimes, and that's why I defend cyber security so much, if I turn it into a crime, an attack on my vulnerabilities, I'll resolve it with my internal bodies, the FBI, the security committee, I don't need the armed forces.

Because when the armed forces come in, especially within the US, they can't act inside the country, by their legislation, by their constitution, the armed forces don't act inside the country, only outside the country, so I can't use the armed forces to defend vulnerabilities. So I realise that it's a crime and I use the FBI and the NSA, the internal instruments of the US federal government. And this reasoning is the same as that found elsewhere.

You didn't mention it there, but Colombia has done a cyber security project, cyber defence, very much based on that of the national police, the federal police here have all the capacity to do security.

So I've divided it up here very clearly, for me it's very clear, the norms of the presidency of the republic. Enforcement and Threat is Defence, Enforcement and Security, the main actor is the Federal Police Alcyon: Got it!!!

Speaker: So when you present cyber defence in Brazil, if you're presenting the military field outside Brazil, Perfect!!! we're just like everyone else.

If you're presenting to a body, despite its name, a communications office and so on, which is a civilian body, it doesn't understand our position. He had G. Thompson here, he had him here and he went to the defence and came to talk to me.

G.Thompson: Explain to me, why are you separated?

Speaker: It's not separate, we're perfectly united, the federal police are together. But institutionally there is no legislation.

We're working because we know each other, but from an institutional point of view Brazil isn't set up like this.

Alcyon: True, because when you talk about the US, there's a higher body that manages both security and defence, ours isn't attached to the presidency...so to speak...

Speaker: It's not aggregated, despite the legislation, free of law, there's only law speaking at this time, the law that constitutes the presidency of the republic and the structure of the presidency, which says that information security is the mission of the gsi. that's law. Everything else is a decree, even the department that was created here, it's not in accordance with the law... But if you take the TCU, it doesn't look at a decree, it looks at the law, the law is the law, the decree is an internal thing, there's only this law that says that information security is the mission of the gsi. Everything else out there isn't law, and it's complicated because my mission, despite the law being there, is for the federal public administration, so if a crime goes outside the public administration, I have no action to protect that information.

In the same way, the federal police can't act, because they can only act in the federal area or if it's a criminal offence, so we have a vacuum in legislation. The same thing when you assign the army to do this kind of thing, they're there to guarantee law and order, so the guarantee of law and order.

When you go to the defence area of other countries, the military area, they understand perfectly, but when you go to a bigger, more complex vision, they don't understand,

Alcyon: What is your perception of the approaches to cyber defence policies by the Brazilian federal public administration?

How are the organisations looking at this, if they are interacting?

Speaker: Lost, I'm the one who understands the general information security committee, dsic, which has the norms, public administration in information security policy, the institutional defence policy, its mission is to take care of military networks and external threats, so it's kind of a bad thing, right, because the guys follow my norms and the strategy on the other side, so what do you have today?

When you have internal conflicts, it's the audit, the TCU audit, that resolves them.

What the TCU says: that the GSI's rules are mandatory, and it couldn't be otherwise because the law only exists here.

So it's a bit confusing. There's even a seminar taking place in a fortnight' time at the army's headquarters.

Look at the Snolden case, they've brought together seven ministers to resolve a soft issue.

And that's not even a problem.

Alcyon: So far nothing has come of it

Speaker: We know what he did. And if we don't know, we're wrong. Alcyon: Anyone could have done it.

Alcyon: Do you think that there are any issues addressed and other cyber security policies that would be relevant to Brazilian politics?

Speaker:

In the Green Book, I think it covers everything that we already knew at the time about what was happening in the world and which is still going on today.

I'm very proud to say that I helped build the Green Book and that it was used to build Colombia's security policy

I would say today with all sincerity, we owe nothing to anyone.

In terms of knowledge, we're on a par with the rest of the world, but in terms of financial resources we're not, and neither is the understanding of our authorities. Brazil has gone 150 years without a war, and people don't understand the need for security and defence.

Alcyon: It's something that's already been said, right, Brazil needs a war... to give it a makeover.

Speaker: Unfortunately...it is unfortunately

Alcyon: According to your experience, are there any national policy guidelines that shouldn't be in your composition?

Speaker: No, I don't think so, it's well rounded, because it's been a long time in the making, for cyber defence, understanding the concepts of security and defence, it doesn't cover all aspects, it doesn't cover crimes, for example.

Alcyon: As an expert on the subject, how do you see the directives for combating cyber-terrorism and cyber-crime, with a view to securing local actors such as companies and civilians?

Speaker: Direct combat... this is a serious problem, what do you notice... who are you going to fight?

There's a book by Patricia Peck that I love that says: Don't make your mouse a weapon, the victim could be you. So you see, if you retaliate to an attack, you can get hurt, because the attack isn't necessarily coming from the computer that's attacking you, usually it's not. So it's a bit tricky to counter-attack, because the moment you counter-attack, at some point, as is being discussed in NATO, it's an act of war, because you're going to attack other countries' servers.

There is an American view that the internet has no borders and that it can use even kinetic force to defend itself.

There's a Russian view, for example, that no, if the server is on my territory, I'm in charge here.

So there are four visions in the world that are opposing each other and have not yet been resolved. And I've already taken part in two events, two groups at the UN, appointed by the UN Secretary General, we worked on each one for a year and a half, and in the end we came to the conclusion that this issue is very important and must continue, and it still hasn't been resolved.

Alcyon: The importance of creating an international body, or one that takes responsibility for this, or one that goes...

Speaker: We have a romantic view that the internet should be international, but the Americans have made every effort and invented the internet as a weapon of war. Do you really think he's going to release it to other countries?

That they're going to build another internet? 80 per cent of the traffic goes through there. You know, it's a crazy business. You're going to force Telefónica, for example, to route all its messages through Africa, while it gets 30% of the cost alone and a 70% discount if it goes through the United States. Who's going to pay for the rest? You see, there's a lot at stake here, and it's not a simple thing to resolve.

Alcyon: Very interesting indeed. How can respect for an individual's right to privacy be addressed by a cyber security policy?

Speaker: I think that Brazil is innovating on this point, with the Civil Rights Framework for the Internet. The Civil Rights Framework is an important point for the rest of the world, there's a lot that I think is nice in the Civil Rights Framework for the Internet, but from the point of view of those who operate the law, it's complicated.

So Congress is there to regulate, which is good for the country, but advances individual rights a lot, on the other hand, it's going to put a stop to electronic and cyber crime and I think it's Congress that has to regulate this.

Alcyon: Let them sort it out. What about the inclusion of cyber defence in combat simulation exercises and joint operations involving federal public administration bodies?
That's why I ask this question about this guideline being included in Brazilian policy, and not in other policies, and has there been a focus on this part of the SMDC, the issue of mobilisation, the creation of war games that teach this, I see that Brazil has a lot, it's the only country that is focusing on this part.

Speaker: I'll put it better to you. It's the only country that is making this explicit.
Which I think is rubbish. You don't have to say that because it's something everyone does. Look, I was taking part in an event organised by the US Department of Defence, Latin America simulation, we run exercises at the OAS, there's a group there to combat cyber-terrorism, there's one in Brazil that's been running this group for nine years, and we run simulations all over Latin America, but that's not a policy, I don't think it's a policy, but it's been put in place.

Alcyon: It would be an arm of a guideline... maybe, right?
Speaker: It's a guideline but it's not explicit, in my opinion, even though everyone does it

Alcyon: To your knowledge, is the creation and maintenance of situational awareness about risk in cyberspace as a guideline for a security policy relevant to the creation of a cybersecurity culture?
That's a point that only South Africans make

Speaker: I think, and I've been arguing for this, that cyber security, information security, information space security should be included. It doesn't matter what it's called because it doesn't have a taxonomy, it hasn't been recognised anywhere yet.

So I think this should start at school, the Mec should play a very big role

I've been trying to talk to the Mec, but there are so many priorities, but I think we have to get there. And this awareness won't just reach me, it has to reach the student, it has to reach the entrepreneur, the micro-entrepreneur.

I was reading a magazine this week and I saw something that sounds like a joke, but it's true: the big problem for businesses, micro-businesses, today in terms of keeping up with taxes is that most entrepreneurs don't know how to use a computer.

It's in one of those weekly magazines, 50% default rate, saying that things have to be paid by boleto, by carnet. There's no point talking about cyber security when the guy doesn't even know how to pay a bill on his computer.

Alcyon: There's a phrase that Patricia Pecker says, in a lecture I attended of hers, about the story that when you're little you show...your father used to say: son, don't accept bullets from strangers, but nobody told us...at least in my generation...My son doesn't open emails from strangers, so the culture really has to come from back then.

Alcyon: One of the guidelines of the Brazilian cyber defence policy is the identification of individual and organisational competences, seeking partnerships and exchanges of cyber experience. Is this action important for the development of the cyber sector in Brazil's federal public administration?

And are there any risks involved in bringing in these private and civil partners?

Speaker: I don't think there's any risk, that's the way forward, we have to involve everyone. Now I don't think it has to be in cyber defence policy.
Cyber security policy is lacking. Defence must focus on

responding to an attack. And preparing if Brazil is attacked, so that it can defend itself, or counter-attack, or an active defence, shouldn't be prepared with security, with crimes, that's not the Ministry of Defence's problem, it's the Ministry of Justice's problem, that's the Ministry of Communications' problem, and this interaction with the Ministry of Development and Commerce, you know it has to take care of companies, there's the Ministry of Science and Technology, we have an agriculture that is becoming more and more computerised, so this is a much bigger issue than just defence. I think it's interesting and it has to be. At the technical level, there's the Gsi, we have 18 standards that range from information security policy to what cryptography to use.

There's an assessment in Sunday's Estadão, talking about the Snolden recording, so here's the thing, it exists on 14 August, we're here, together with Gsi, Dsic, Abin, in the auditorium showing 2 tools for protection, including encrypted telephone, encrypted desk phone, who uses this, only MRE, Defence, ABIN and the Federal Police, only others don't use it,

Alcyon: And they don't even care

Lecturer: Then there's that story about being cashed in at war again

One thing I even see in the matter of taxonomy, in the academic papers and publications themselves, people confuse defence and security a lot, they think it's the same thing, cyber defence policy itself was born as cyber security, which is why I talk about cyber security and cyber defence in my work.

Speaker: I think Mangabeira has done a fantastic job on the national defence strategy, even though he has no knowledge of this area, he's brilliant, he knows everything, but he doesn't have in-depth knowledge of this area, what he designed there is over, but this has to come down, we have to have the vision that it's not the same thing, committing an international crime over the internet for example, is quite different from an attack on Brazil's critical infrastructure, and we have to understand the role of each one, even institutional. Personally, I hate to see the army making roads in the middle of the street, I don't think it's their role, but the national situation wants the army to do it, is that the mission?! Don't we have to think about that?

Alcyon: I wasn't supposed to be involved.

Speaker: Is it the role of the army to carry out cyber security, especially in an area where the hierarchy is worthless?

If you have an accident, the corporal in front of the computer can't ask the sergeant, he can't ask the lieutenant, he can't ask anyone, he has to act. In actions that are parameterised, it's a certainty that the top is going to act, and anything that goes off the rails, I doubt that the soldiers and combatants are going to consult their superiors.

This is an issue in the armed forces, it's not a modus operandi, this is basic in the armed forces, so I think there's a vacuum there that needs to be filled, I say this in every lecture.

We work together, the Ministry of Defence, Dsic, and the Pf, these are the three pillars of this area, and these three things work together, the link is not institutional, I have direct contact with the lieutenants.

Alcyon: If it depended on that, there would be no communication at all.

Speaker: Look, formally I don't have any communication channels with these people. We talk because we know what we have to do and the three of them know each other and have been at it for a long time. Now one of their legs has changed and they think differently, it's over, the link will be broken. Because if it's through an institutional channel, how long will it take?!!?

So there is no body to do this.

I continue to argue that there is a need for a body to do this... The creation of a body, a ministry, an agency, a national secretariat for this, something that has the operators, that formalises the contact between the various players in this link.

The first time I spoke about cyber security in the federal government was in October 2006, when the president was the current minister of the civil house. I remember it was the most embarrassing silence of my life, and when I finished there was no reaction.

Alcyon: Maybe people got scared

No, I think it was something so out of touch with Brazilian reality at the time, in 2006, when it came to information security, that people were sensitised to creating the Green Book and came to study it more here. But it was something so far off the beaten track, from what they were used to, that cyber security...is that important?!!?

People had an idea of critical infrastructure, they had an idea of information security, but they didn't see the Internet as a critical infrastructure, which wasn't tangible, it was a very complicated thing to understand, and I'm not talking about a long time ago, I'm talking about seven years ago,

Alcyon: There were already many fronts running in another country, right?

Speaker: The United States had already started working on it, Germany and England only. And Russia was starting on what they called the Information Protection Programme

Alcyon: They were talking in error too, right?

Speaker: No no, maybe because of the language, maybe because of the culture, for example they don't have Astronauts, they have Cosmonauts.

They don't have cybernetic, they have informational, that protection isn't space but information, it's a cultural issue that one day they'll sort out somewhere.

Alcyon: The question of international cooperation

I'd like to know what you think about the issue of international cooperation, whether it's important for the development of cyber defence and why.

Because Brazilian politics is the only one that doesn't address this

Speaker: With all due respect, everything has a political context, a political context is always loaded with ideology, so we have a policy, which is a state policy but has an ideological bias embedded in it, not least because we are in a democratic country, with political views, and that's part of the game.

I'm sure that international cooperation is fundamental, we have to have this cooperation, because nobody knows how to defend themselves against this alone, nobody can defend themselves against this alone, nobody has the methodology, a real thing..............

Alcyon: Like a cake recipe

Speaker: No, there isn't, so everyone is learning from everyone else, I think that because of Brazil's tradition, we shouldn't adopt a bloc policy, nor a multilateral one, Brazil has a tradition of bilateral agreements in this area and ....

Alcyon: It's funny that even at the table discussion that took place now at Consegi, which I took part in, in the lecture given by a colonel who I can't remember now, it was said that this co-operation already existed before this policy was signed...

Speaker: We're at a time when Brazil is favouring Mercosur, and nothing is going to come of it. This cyber defence, cyber security adventure, but then you can't invent these things again here because it's not just happening here, it's happening all over the world, so we have to cooperate with other countries in America as well.

You see strange things like that, a country like Iran was attacked, at the same time Georgia was attacked, Estonia was attacked, there was a blackout in Italy that affected the whole of Europe, so these things are no longer about geopolitics, so it's a bit exempt from engemonia

But I don't think it was a matter of forgetting, there was a view that this subject shouldn't be dealt with in strategy, because it wasn't something that was very popular with all the members of the government, at the same time as the part of the military exercise, at that time which helped with the projection of power, it would be important to put this here...

Alcyon: What's your view on...the approach to what the table asked...we've actually gone further...the good thing about the structured interview is that...we can navigate.

Is the training of specialised technical personnel in the cyber sector important for the development of the federal public administration sector?

Speaker: As a whole, it's important as a whole, Brazil today doesn't have enough network administrators, it doesn't have enough people with security composure, this is much more of the federal public administration, 6,000 public bodies, 1.6 million civil servants, most of them with a computer in front of them, all using mobile phones, pen drives, and counting the many outsourced workers, many fourth parties, and sometimes the security manager is held hostage by the government, nothing against the outsourced worker, any point of policy must be analysed.

Alcyon: It's in M04, information security can't be in the hands of any outsourcer

Speaker: Then you realise that the reality is different, now you need to have a precise culture... I'm on my fourth management course, specialising in information security, I'm doing this course for civil servants who have a stable career and will stay in government, they're going to graduate now when they finish 600, and not everyone stays in the area, the military have a military culture that they're going to transfer, so they're here today and tomorrow they could be exchanging fire on the border. Alcyon: That's true.

Speaker: That's true in every organisation, the guy has taken over as head of administration for I don't know what. He's head of protocol, and then ....that. ....

There's no career, I don't know if it's good or not.

There's no telling whether the guy will stay in the area or not, it's an area that requires a lot of knowledge, a lot of co-operation, and there aren't enough training schools for that.

The certifications that exist are specific, and they run out soon, and I wanted to broaden this offer, My goal is to reach 1% of the civil service, that would be 1400.
When I started there were 900 civil servants

Alcyon: I know you're pressed for time, but...a doctor was talking in a fantastic interview about the invasion of Snolden, going back to this.... thing.

He said that it's an area for the few and not for the willing.

Speaker: You have to have a vision...A guy like Snolden must be very well prepared, but to me he's a crook, no matter what his intention, he stole information, which wasn't his...no matter how good his intention, he wasn't patriotic, so if he doesn't have confidence in his country what confidence do I have in this guy?!!!

Who says that the data is real or that he hasn't manipulated it?

Alcyon: There's still that point... Nobody knows if it's true.
Speaker: What's the point?!?! Could it be that the NSA didn't publicise it on purpose?!!? To show strength,

I think that this area of Information Security is a very sensitive area, and should follow the Italian Intelligence model, where nobody goes into the intelligence area... people are invited. With the exception of Brazil and Angola, which have public tenders, which people think is crazy, but in the rest of the world, people are recruited to the intelligence area.

And this area of information security should also be recruited, I don't trust, I don't believe, nobody will prove to me, that a hacker is a guy who can work in this area... he can't. I've never seen a door-knocker called to be a locksmith. I don't understand...

At the time I said this, I was even beaten up by the newspapers and so on, even Kaspersky said the same thing, that he doesn't work for hackers in his company, because hackers are crooks.

Then I said, "Oh... my displeasure, coming from a big thug... If he's a thug, no...".
hires, because he started his life and he knows, he knows his colleagues...
So I think that training is a fundamental loss, and it really is, and it's not for everyone.

one, so the guy has to have a very strong moral structure... I'll give you an example here.

We have a Network Incident Centre here, which is the federal government's centre, when I started here with Dsic, Serpro, Bacen, BB and Inss I think, there were about 5 to 6, today there are about 200 that we've managed to substantiate... So the guys resolve them there and when they don't, they move up.

Serpro has people all over Brazil, regional scales, national scales, and if there's a problem it comes here, I have 60 error notifications, it comes in the filter, it comes, and there are 60 different ones, so here only the bone arrives, not even meat, only the bone arrives, and here things like...look, the authority had its mobile phone hacked, and there were private photos and stuff...you know...man it's something that brings down the government.

Alcyon: Yes, right away.

Speaker: So I only have the military, the intelligence officers, the federal police and the proclaimer of the republic working with me. Why ?!!? because they have to be people who have mass blood security. I put a girl here, I'm not going to say her name, halfway through the first day, she was in the cafeteria commenting on all the things that were appearing there, analysing pornographic films, but there was malware embedded in there, so what do people think?!! like the guy watching pornographic films, so much so that my network is completely segregated from the presidency's network, and it has to be, because how am I going to get a virus through the presidency's network, I contaminate everything.

Alcyon: You're going to be a disseminator, right?

Speaker: So for a guy to work in this area he has to have a different vision. And I joke with the people who work there that they have the right: to have time to come in, to sunbathe for 1 hour a day, and they only leave when they've finished 60 OS for the day. And that's how it has to be because 60 more are due tomorrow, so they can't finish. So it's a difficult area to work in, it's not just technical preparation.

Alcyon: It's more complex, right, even the question of analysing...

Speaker: So much so that there was a young man who was selected, passed the Abin, went into the IT area, he started stealing information.

He's a guy who, in his heart of hearts, wasn't one for it.

He was arrested, had a case brought against him, and did what he did out of curiosity. And there's no such thing as curiosity in this area.

Alcyon: Curiosity is very strong, right?

Speaker: Now I'm sure if the guy was recruited, he could do the same thing, but he'd be much better prepared.

Alcyon: That makes it difficult...

Speaker: Today you take a public examination, pass the selection and that's it.

You do a psychotechnical test, and you check the guy's social psyche, you no longer have the power of decision... this guy won't get in...

Alcyon: It's complicated, it's between a rock and a hard place.

Speaker: Democracy looks cool

Alcyon: But there's a downside to that, right, the control points as they say.

Alcyon: Based on your experience, what would be the best way of coordinating cyber security? The sectors responsible for coordinating their defence strategies would be directly subordinated to a responsible body, in this case, the idea would be to create a central body from which defence and security would come?

Speaker: A normative body. And this body should be in the book of the presidency of the republic. And the executive already exists, which is the Federal Police, the Army, the big network operators, Bacen, you know...Serpro, I think, the body, it should be a normative body, and this normative body should not be from the federal public administration, it should be from Brazilian society, because look, today any guy who does this here, breaks the government's network, whether he's a civil servant or not, it's

just log in to Bolsa Família and send a virus.

Today, the companies protect themselves inside the walls, and what gets there?!?! electricity, water, telephony, where's their protection?!! it's in another company?!! and the other companies, if you remember, there are no national telecoms companies, they're all foreign...

Alcyon: Only Telebrás is...and even then not....

Speaker: Even so, you don't have the last mile, you don't answer the phone.

Alcyon: It's only for the government Speaker: It is Speaker: And it doesn't matter, the United States doesn't have any national ones either, now the rules that exist are complied with, whereas our rules aren't complied with, our legislation is flawed...

We need someone to think about this. Because project 3505 is the first, national political plan that talks about information security, creates information security policy 03 June 2000, I've said this so much that I even know the date...In 2000 this story was thought up, in 2000 I was in the group that started to create CGSI, from all the ministries, there were 16 at the time, the IT guys, it was still IT at the time, soon after it evolved and there had to be a body, to make it happen the group meets once a month and thinks about what it's going to do, 1 DSIC was missing, and it came about 6 years later, and after that we have 6 internalised standards in Brazil, and we didn't invent anything, we wrote it, Iso....

Alcyon: A 27002

Lecturer:There's something that sounds like an exchange of words but it's true, we as citizens can do anything that isn't prohibited by law, this is a Brazilian right, a universal right. A civil servant can only do what is allowed, if it's not in the law he can't do it, so when you tell a guy to do information security following 2007, he can do it if he wants, even if it's an ABNT standard, it's not a government standard, so you have to take that standard and translate it into the civil service. When I issue a standard here, look, this standard now belongs to the government, it has to be complied with, the person responsible is the main manager, because until then the guy could recommend the guy to do Iso 2007, but he could be a politician, and politicians are only afraid of one thing, becoming ineligible.

So that would be my great contribution, working together with the TCU, each in their own square, but the TCU recognising that my rules have to be enforced, and holding the top manager accountable, because since August last year information security has ceased, or should have ceased, to be an IT concern and has become

of the strategic link, as it should be...

Somehow information security, we only talk about cybernetics, and I keep saying that defence is one thing and security, and information security is another, because this is information, it does and I don't know what, and people forget, it's the cupboard written like this, Secret Documents, with the key on the door, so it's this culture that people lack, even the security people don't have this habit, and this culture I   have

a few words that for me are watchwords, to end our conversation here.

Capacity building, collaboration and coordination are words that I think are key to thinking about cyber security, defence, information security and whatever else you can think of.

Training, because today there's more information technology on board at the gate than there was in 1976 when I started in IT, or data processing as they call it now, any little badge nowadays has more technology than it used to, and nowadays it's still the same, You put your hand through the turnstile, you get access, you see the poorly trained guard, he still has the same view of organic security, he doesn't really know what's going on in front of him, you can tell the guy to ban everything that's on a USB stick, a child comes in with a little USB stick in his hand, and you can't take his head off.... he doesn't even think about it.

Collaboration because nowadays nobody works alone, even the United States, the strongest country in the world, can't work alone...

Coordination because today actions are prioritised, so agents have to coordinate these actions...

END

ANNEX 1

Mandarino Júnior and Canongia (2009) present a demonstration of the US and UK recommendations for the National Cyber Security Strategy adopted by those nations, a table that characterises a brief summary of the views of the author of this article.

USA	United Kingdom
Creation of an integrated and detailed US national security strategy for cyberspace	**Developing the UK's cyber security strategy**
The government should adjust the current	The UK's first National Cyber Security

strategy and establish an integrated and detailed National Cyberspace Security Strategy, in which macro-coordination is carried out by a body/agency specifically created for this purpose within the White House. This body would promote the proper synergy of the issue, primarily in the diplomatic sphere in terms of international insertion, the military sphere in terms of doctrine and planning, the economic sphere in terms of policy, intelligence in its activities, and legal frameworks in terms of updating and dynamising them;	Strategy, launched in June 2009, has the following objectives: • establish an intra-governmental and inter-governmental programme in priority areas of cyber security, providing additional funds for research, development and innovation (R,D&I), as well as for the development and promotion of critical skills and competences; • closer cooperation between the public sector and the private sector, non and international partners; • create a specific central body, in this case the Office Cyber Security (0CS), to provide the necessary leadership and macro coordination; e, • create a specific operational body,
	in this case the Cyber Security Operations Centre (CS0C), to primarily monitor cyberspace and coordinate responses to incidents, establish better conditions of understanding and knowledge about cyber attacks against UK networks and users, and provide information about the risks, both for commercial transactions and businesses, and for the public sector with regard to cyberspace.
Organisation of national structures for cyber security The President should establish within the National Security Council (NSC) a Cyber	**New government structures for cyber action** 0 government will establish the *Office of Cyber Security (OCS),* which will work within the *Cabinet Office,* and will be the body

Security Directorate that would absorb the functions currently carried out by the Homeland Security Council (HSC). In addition, the new National Cyberspace Agency should support the work of the new NSC Cyber Security Directorate, and should act as the President's direct advisor on this matter. The President should also promote the merger between the existing National Cyber Security Centre (NCSC) and the Joint Inter-Agency Cyber Task Force (JJACTF - created by the National Intelligence Director). The Department of Homeland Security should also establish the National Cyber Security Centre (NCSC).	responsible for the strategic leadership of the issue, promoting greater synergy and macro-coordination of the various government programmes towards cyber security, without duplication of effort, but with due prioritisation of national objectives in the area. 0 government will also establish a multi-agency, the *Cyber Security Operations Centre (CSOC),* to monitor cyber space, analyse trends, and strengthen the coordination of technical responses to cyber incidents. 0 CS0C will also be responsible for
Homeland Security (DHS) should remain responsible for the United States Computer Emergency Readiness Team (US-CERT) as well as the respective US-CERT Einstein Programme.	disseminate information to government, industry and international partners on the risks and opportunities of cyber security. The new structures will be established in September 2009 and put into effective operation by the end of March 2010.
Partnerships with the private sector The US government should "rebuild" public-private partnerships in cybersecurity in order to focus on the nation's key/critical infrastructures. To this end, an Advisory Committee should be formed to act at presidential level, with senior representatives from key/critical cyber infrastructures. In this sense, this new Committee should incorporate both the National Security and Telecommunications Advisory Committee (NSTAC) and the National Infrastructure Advisory Council (NIAC).	**Defence, security and resistance system** 0 government will focus on preparing for and protecting against cyber attacks in all sectors, providing greater resilience and response. To this end, it will endeavour to increase understanding of potential vulnerabilities and impacts, as well as to develop appropriate mitigation measures.

Regulating cyber security The new National Cybersecurity Body/Agency should develop a macro-coordination on the aspects of security norms and standards for critical cyber infrastructure, so that the different regulatory agencies in the country can coordinate their work.	**Policy, doctrine and legal and regulatory frameworks** The new Office of Cyber Security (OCS) will identify gaps in current doctrine, policy, legislation and regulation through a framework that points to the domestic and international landscape.
have their activities aligned with the common goal of cyber security	the development of specific policies and promote greater interaction within the government, as well as the development and implementation of the industrial cyber security strategy, in close collaboration with key industry players. Thus, strengthening partnerships with the private sector will be key to sustaining and promoting national capabilities in this area and stimulating innovation. For the development of the legal and regulatory framework, such partnerships will also be essential, in addition to working closely with the actors and bodies that have such competences and scope of action.
Security in industrial control systems and SCADA (Supervisory Control and Data Acquisition) The new National Cybersecurity Body/Agency should work together with the appropriate regulatory agencies and the National Institute for Standards and Technology (NIST) to develop security standards, technical regulations and metrological standards for the certification of industrial control systems.	Understanding and culture The new Office of Cyber Security (0CS) will lead the work of broadening the understanding and strengthening the culture of cyber security, identifying and changing It will also prioritise the various aspects related to cyber security in the formulation of the policy. Among the measures is the

	development of risk-based decision-making. This practice represents a substantial
	It will require specific work to ensure that the right and consistent information arrives at the right time and in the right hands, in order to guarantee more effective and efficient decision-making in the sensitive field of cyber security.
Strengthening security in the acquisition and use of IT services and products The new National Cyber Security Body/Agency should work in close partnership with the private sector to establish a basic guide for the acquisition and use of information technology, paying special attention to software. In addition, efforts to increase Internet security should be prioritised, including, among the necessary actions, the development of mandatory technical regulations for Internet security protocols. This measure should also be part of an international articulation strategy for Internet security.	**Skills and education** 0 government will examine the requirements and steps needed to develop the capacities, skills and training of cyber security specialists to work in government and industry. It will not limit itself to the technical aspects required, but rather to combining different approaches and covering the existing gaps in this field. Training, incentives for certification and specific career development will be developed for work inside and outside government.
Management and accreditation The system for authenticating identities should be strengthened, especially for those people who work at	**Technical, research and development (R&D) capacities** 0 government will make significant contributions to the work of updating the doctrine, policy, legal and regulatory frameworks.
critical cyber infrastructure (ICT, energy, finance, essential government services). In addition, the adoption of the Common Identification Standard Policy for Employees and Contractors within the US Federal Government, in accordance with the Homeland	and the implementation of the cyber security strategy in industry, with an emphasis on critical national infrastructures such as health, energy and others. To this end, R&D efforts and prioritisation will promote better effects, especially when considering the international

Security Presidential Directive: HSPD-12, should be strongly emphasised. In addition, government accreditation should also support consumers in online activities, while respecting the rights of individual privacy and civil liberty.	partnerships taking place in academia. In the first instance, additional resources will be allocated to support and expand collaborative work to protect government and industrial networks. The new Office of Cyber Security (0CS) will also work in strong co-operation with the Network Security Innovation Platform (NSIP) on the Technology Strategy Board, aiming to provide opportunities for UK high-tech companies.
Modernisation	**Exploitation**
The President, together with the Ministry of Justice, should re-examine the statutes and processes for investigating cyber-crimes, in order to make them clearer, more agile, and with better protection of privacy. At the same time, it should release a basic guide with indications of circumstances and requirements for the use and enforcement of the law, as well as the use of military and intelligence authorities in cyber incidents.	The United Kingdom will develop actions to understand and identify the necessary capabilities and competences to exploit cyber space, in order to combat threats from criminals, terrorists and other actors, through effective and efficient work to combat cyber attacks, providing due defence of national interests and society.
Revision of the Federal Information Security Management Act (FISMA 2002) The President should work with Congress to "rewrite" the Federal Information Security Management Act - 2002 (FISMA), the US information security regulatory framework of the National Institute of Standards and Technology (NIST), so that it includes aspects of cyber security.	International engagement The new Office of Cyber Security (OCS) will be responsible for building the coherence and synergy of the UK's cyber security work vis-à-vis the policies, strategies and best practices of international partners and organisations. At first, the OCS will not be part of the numerous bilateral and multilateral agreements that each agency or body already has in place. Rather, it will exercise macro-coordination of these activities in order to develop a single UK vision and message on cyber security, aligned with the visions of strategic allies, and making itself

	present in international commissions and forums.
Eliminate the division between civilian and national security guidelines and standards 0 President should propose legislation that eliminates the existing distinction between technical security standards and regulations for national systems and those of civilian agencies, adopting a risk-based approach.	**Governance, roles and responsibilities** UK governance will be modelled for all aspects related to cyber security, developing a theoretical framework that includes lessons learned, best practices, key partners and the change initiatives required. One of the critical areas, that of cyber crime, will require a brief review of the roles and responsibilities of the actors directly involved, as well as
	of the strategic requirements, under the leadership and macro-coordination of the OCS, to ensure the UK's National Cyber Security Strategy. This recommendation also includes intra-government efforts to promote and prioritise the National Cyber Security Strategy, which will involve the participation and collaboration of stakeholders, non-governmental bodies and society.
Training and education in cybernetics and workforce development The President should, through the new Cyber Security Agency, and working together with government training and personnel management agencies, create training programmes for government activities in the field of cyber. He should also work with the National Science Foundation (NSF) to develop a national education programme on the subject.	
Research and development (R&D) in	

cybernetics 0 new Cyber Security Body/Agency, working together with the Office of Science and Technology Policy	
(OSTP), should carry out macro-coordination of R&D in cybernetics.	

ANNEX 2

Defence Cyber Policy
NORMATIVE ORDINANCE No. 3.389/MD, OF
21 DECEMBER 2012

Provides for the Cyber Defence Policy. THE MINISTER OF STATE FOR DEFENCE, in the use of the powers conferred on him by item II of the sole paragraph of art. 87 of the Constitution, and having regard to the provisions of items III, VI and IX of art. 1º and item VII of art. 16 of Annex I of Decree no. 7.364, of 23 November 2010, and Decree no. 6.703, of 18 December 2008, resolves:

Art. 1 Approve the Defence Cyber Policy - MD31-P-02 (1ª Edition/2012), attached to this Normative Order.

Art. 2 This Ordinance comes into force on the date of its publication.

CELSO AMORIM

ANNEX

CYBER DEFENCE POLICY

CHAPTER I
INTRODUCTION

1.1. Purpose

The purpose of the Cyber Defence Policy is to guide, within the Ministry of Defence (MD), Cyber Defence activities at the strategic level and Cyber Warfare activities at the operational and tactical levels, with a view to achieving their objectives.

1.2. Application

The Cyber Defence Policy applies to all components of the military expression of National Power, as well as to entities that may participate in Defence or Cyber Warfare activities.

1.3. Basic assumptions

The objectives and guidelines of the Cyber Defence Policy are defined according to the following basic assumptions:

a) the effectiveness of Cyber Defence actions depends fundamentally on the collaborative action of Brazilian society, including not only the MD, but also the academic community, the public and private sectors and the defence industrial base;
b) the MD's Cyber Defence activities are geared towards meeting the needs of National Defence;

c) offensive cyber actions must comply with the planning drawn up in accordance with the Hypotheses of Employment (HE);
d) the technological training of the Cyber Sector must be pursued in harmony with the Science, Technology and Innovation Policy for National Defence (S,T&I);
e) the effectiveness of the MD's Cyber Defence actions depends directly on the degree of awareness achieved among organisations and individuals of the value of the information they hold or process;
f) Information and Communications Security (ICS) is the basis of Cyber Defence and depends directly on individual actions; there is no Cyber Defence without ICS actions; and g) cyber actions in the context of the MD aim to ensure the use of cyberspace, preventing or hindering its use against the interests of the country and thus guaranteeing freedom of action.

CHAPTER II
THE OBJECTIVES

2.1. Objectives

The objectives of the Cyber Defence Policy are:
a) jointly ensuring the effective use of cyberspace (preparation and operational use) by the Armed Forces (AF) and preventing or hindering its use against the interests of National Defence; or hindering its use against the interests of National Defence;
b) to train and manage the human talent needed to conduct the activities of the Cyber Sector (St Cyber) within the MD;
c) to collaborate in the production of intelligence knowledge from cyber sources of interest to the Defence Intelligence System (SINDE) and to government bodies involved in CIS and Cyber Security, in particular the Office of Institutional Security of the Presidency of the Republic (GSI/PR);
d) develop and keep up-to-date the doctrine for the use of St Cyber;
e) implement measures that contribute to SIC Management within the MD;
f) adapting the S,T&I structures of the three Forces and implementing research and development activities to meet the needs of St Cyber;
g) define the basic principles that will guide the creation of specific legislation and standards for employment in St Cyber;
h) cooperate with the national and military mobilisation effort to ensure the operational capacity and, consequently, the deterrent capacity of St Cyber; and
i) contribute to the security of the information assets of the Federal Public Administration (FPA), with regard to Cyber Security, located outside the scope of the MD.

CHAPTER III

THE GUIDELINES

3.1. Definition

The guidelines explain the activities to be implemented by the MD to achieve the objectives set out in the Defence Cyber Policy.

3.2. Guidelines

3.2.1. Guidelines for Objective No. I - to jointly ensure the effective use of cyberspace (preparation

and operational use) by the Armed Forces (AF) and to prevent or hinder its use against the interests of National Defence:
a)   design and implement the Military Cyber Defence System (SMDC), with the participation of military personnel from the FA and civilians;
b)   create a structure to coordinate and integrate St Cyber within the scope of the MD, as the central body of the SMDC, with the possibility of participation by AF military personnel and civilians;
c)   to survey the critical information infrastructures associated with St Cyber in order to contribute to the formation of the situational awareness necessary for Cyber Defence activities;
d)   establish risk criteria inherent in information assets,
and manage them, reducing the risks to critical information infrastructures of interest to National Defence to acceptable levels;
e)   create and standardise Cyber Security processes to standardise accreditation procedures within the scope of critical information infrastructures of interest to National Defence; and
f)   establishing programmes/projects to ensure the capacity to operate securely in a network, thus strengthening the operationality of the Command and Control (C2) activity in the MD.

3.2.2.   Guidelines for Objective II - to train and manage the human talent needed to conduct St Cyber activities within the MD:
a)   define the profiles of the personnel needed to carry out St Cyber's activities;
b)   create specific positions and functions and furnish them with specialised personnel to meet St Ciber's needs;
c)   establish criteria and control the mobilisation and demobilisation of personnel for Cyber Defence activities;
d)   identifying, registering and selecting personnel with competences or skills from the AF's internal and external environments to join the SMDC;
e)   Continuously train personnel to work in St Cyber, under the guidance of the SMDC's central body, making use of existing structures;
f)   make it possible for staff involved with St Ciber to take part in courses, internships, congresses, seminars, symposia and other similar activities in Brazil and abroad;
g)   periodically hold events to present and discuss relevant topics in areas of interest to the Cyber Sector, to be organised and led by the SMDC's central body, in order to level up and update knowledge;
h)   create instruments to enable and motivate the retention of specialised staff in St Ciber's activities, allowing the continuity of the activity;
i)   strategic partnerships and exchanges between the FA and institutions of interest; and
j)   to include Cyber Defence content in the curricula of courses at all levels, where appropriate, of the MD's educational establishments.

3.2.3.   Guidelines for Objective III - to collaborate in the production of intelligence knowledge from cyber sources of interest to SINDE and to government bodies involved in CIS and Cyber Security, especially the GSI/PR:

a)   adapting intelligence doctrine to include the cyber source in the context of integrating data sources with a view to producing knowledge;
b)   create Cyber Intelligence structures, according to the
the need for the central intelligence bodies of the FA and the SMDC to apply scientific and systematic methods in order to extract and analyse data from the cyber source, producing knowledge of interest;
c)   establishing a systemic/technical channel between the central body of the SMDC and the central intelligence bodies of the FA, within the scope of the SINDE, with regard to St Cyber; and
d)   survey critical information infrastructures associated with internal and external threats, real or potential, to contribute to the formation of the situational awareness necessary for intelligence activities.

3.2.4. Guidelines for Objective N^0 IV - to develop and keep up-to-date the doctrine for the use of St Cyber:
a)   create the Cyber Defence doctrine at the proposal of the SMDC central body;
b)   encourage the development and exchange of theses,
dissertations and other similar works, with a doctrinal focus, in civilian and military higher education institutions of interest to St Cyber's activities;
c)   promote doctrinal, normative and technical exchanges with civilian and military institutions, both national and from friendly nations;
d)   include Cyber Defence in combat simulation exercises and joint operations;
e)   create a knowledge management system of lessons learnt to compose and update the doctrine; and
f)   designate the central body of the SMDC as responsible for proposing innovations and updating doctrine for St Cyber within Defence.

3.2.5. Guidelines for Objective V - implement measures that contribute to SIC Management within the MD:
a)   implement the Defence's SIC Management methodology, taking into account current legislation, standards and best practices,
the Defence Intelligence Doctrine and international standards of interest;
b)   implement a Defence public key infrastructure (ICP Defence);
c)   determine interoperable Defence cryptography standards in addition to those of the AF; and d) implement the Defence SIC audit system.

3.2.6. Guidelines for Objective VI - to adapt the S,T&I structures of the three Forces and implement research and development activities to meet the needs of St Cyber:
a)   plan and execute the adaptation of Science, Technology and Innovation (S,T&I) structures, integrating efforts between the FA to meet the needs of St Cyber;
b)   create a permanent committee within the Defence Department, made up of representatives of the MD and invited guests from other ministries and development agencies, to intensify and explore new opportunities for cooperation in S,T&I in areas of interest to St Cyber;
c)   to prospect the needs of St Cyber, in the area of S,T&I, within the scope of Defence, in order to identify the scientific-technological capacities necessary for the development of the Sector;
d)   identify specific (individual and organisational) competences in S,T&I of interest to St Cyber, within the scope of the MD and civilian research and development centres (public and private), establishing partnerships between centres of excellence at national level, to bring institutions together and avoid the dispersion of resources;

e)   create partnerships and cooperation between military research and development centres and civilian research and development centres (public and private), to encourage the integration of initiatives of interest to St Cyber; and
f)   create programmes within the MD, in partnership with the MCTI, that take into account the dual characteristics (civilian and military use) of the information and communications technologies (ICT) used in the cyber area, to strengthen the involvement of the industrial sector in the development phases of projects of interest to St Cyber.

3.2.7. Guidelines for Objective VII - to define the basic principles that will guide the creation of specific legislation and standards for employment in St Cyber:
a)   collaborate with the body of the Presidency of the Republic (PR) in charge of drawing up the National Cyber Security Policy;
b)   keeping the Defence Cyber Policy up to date in line with the National Cyber Security Policy, when it exists;
c)   define attributions and responsibilities for carrying out activities related to Cyber Defence;
d)   to draw up proposals for the creation and adaptation of federal legislation in order to support

Cyber Defence activities;
e) propose the creation of a budget programme to make St Ciber's actions and activities viable;
f) revise the planning of the Employment Hypotheses (EH) to take account of actions in cyberspace; and
g) proposing the adaptation of the National Mobilisation Law and the National Mobilisation System (SINAMOB) to make them compatible with the needs of St Cyber.

3.2.8. Guidelines for Objective VIII - cooperate with the national and military mobilisation effort to ensure the operational capacity and, consequently, the deterrent capacity of St Cyber:
a) carry out a systematic survey of information assets that can be mobilised for St Cyber;
b) to draw up and keep up to date a database of information assets of interest to the mobilisation in favour of the SMDC;
c) drawing up Information Asset Mobilisation Plans, with the respective costs, in line with the National Mobilisation Law;
d) adapting the SMDC's mobilisation needs to SINAMOB; and
e) to propose to the federal government a national education campaign on Cyber Defence, aimed at National Mobilisation, to raise the level of awareness of Brazilian society.

3.2.9. Guidelines for Objective IX - to contribute to the security of the APF's information assets, with regard to Cyber Security, located outside the MD's scope:
a) to know, through the PR, the critical information infrastructures of the APF bodies located outside the MD;
b) collaborate, within the limits of the legislation in force, with the other agencies of the APF, upon request and through the PR, to re-establish security

Cybernetics;
c) maintain a database and establish a systemic/technical channel between the SMDC central body and the APF bodies for sharing information on network incidents; and d) act in the recognition of artefacts and development of cyber tools, in conjunction with the PR, contributing to the protection of APF information assets.

CHAPTER IV

RESPONSIBILITIES AND UPDATING

4.1. Responsibilities

The Joint Chiefs of Staff of the Armed Forces (EMCFA) is the body responsible for advising the Minister of State for Defence on the implementation and management of the SMDC, with the aim of guaranteeing, within the scope of Defence, the ability to act in a network, the interoperability of systems and the achievement of the desired levels of security.

4.2. Update

This Policy must be reviewed and updated periodically by the MD, through the EMCFA, on its own initiative or at the proposal of one of the Armed Forces.

I want morebooks!

Buy your books fast and straightforward online - at one of world's fastest growing online book stores! Environmentally sound due to Print-on-Demand technologies.

Buy your books online at
www.morebooks.shop

Kaufen Sie Ihre Bücher schnell und unkompliziert online – auf einer der am schnellsten wachsenden Buchhandelsplattformen weltweit! Dank Print-On-Demand umwelt- und ressourcenschonend produzi ert.

Bücher schneller online kaufen
www.morebooks.shop

info@omniscriptum.com
www.omniscriptum.com

Printed by Books on Demand GmbH, Norderstedt / Germany